INTRO

The following pages are an honest account of events between April 2005 and May 2011. They represent a side of the story which is rarely, if ever, heard.

'For Hansel and Gretel'

'Don't go into the woods tonight!'

BUNTING FAR By Crowmarsh Gifford

THE WEDDING FEAST AT CANAAN (OR:

'MY JOURNEY INTO MADNESS')

I'm going to try and work a bloody miracle; I'm going to try to make sense of everything that's happened. Not just for you, but for me as well. There are things which should have been said a long time ago but weren't. Things which *were* said which shouldn't have been, because they were untrue. Nothing I say is meant to embarrass you in any way, but I will have to mention everything which I think will make it all a bit clearer. I need you to understand the truth and not what people who don't know me have said about me. In all the time I knew you did I ever do anything deliberately to hurt you?

I know you tried to ring me several times, but I just couldn't pick up the phone. I'm not sure why. I never found it easy to talk to you. It seemed easier to keep you in suspense.

I once gave you a piece of paper with ten things I wanted to discuss with you written down. When I came back from the kitchen it was tossed down the side of the sofa as if it was of no importance. You said you had read it, but you didn't make any comment. Words are important to me. I prefer to express myself through words. Some of what you read may be a bit distressing. I am sorry about that, but I just want you to understand what you have done, and why I did what I did. Some things are very hard to talk about...as time's gone on you must have had a lot of experiences I haven't been a part of, but there are many questions which still need to be answered. Trying to make sense of the terrible sequence of events which followed may actually make them more bearable. Surely all this suffering can't have been for nothing...?

I may have strained the boundaries somewhat, and I do tend to challenge authority, but I have never been an unpleasant or malicious person. The trials which followed were as a result of my mischievous nature, my habit of taking risks, my temptation to bend the rules, and to question everything.

I can't begin to say how sorry I am about how affairs have ended up. I am truly sorry for all the hurt and upheaval I have caused you, but you can't go through the rest of your life believing what is wrong about me. I'm not perfect. I know I have a devilish streak, and I have done a lot of things I haven't been proud of, but you only have to scratch the surface to find your *Guardian angel*.

There are lots of things I would change if I could do.

When I met you I never wanted you to think I was anything other than a decent caring thoughtful gentleman.

Please read what I have to say carefully, in private, quietly, without any interference from anyone else.

When we first met you seemed very vulnerable and withdrawn. I drove across in the work van and kissed you through the window (your cheek was very soft). I recognised your voice from the phone. You were saying goodnight to some Solicitor friends. I couldn't stay very long. It was already dark. You told me to say we had met on a course in the Health service. You were working as a Health Visitor. One of your clients was Tim Henman. Your work involved reporting any poor dysfunctional families who lived in the shacks up the road, even when physical or sexual abuse was only faintly suspected. A part of your job description which you performed with relish and enthusiasm.

You complained later about the times I came over. It was quieter in the evenings at work and it was the only time I could really get away. Another reason is because I find it a lot more peaceful and relaxing after the sun has gone down and when there aren't so many people around. I contacted you because you lived close by

and I felt like some fresh company.
You seemed a bit straight up and down. Not very curvy.

You were very different to anyone I had ever known before.
The second time we met you invited me in and we cuddled on the sofa. You sent me a message on my way across which read... 'in lust...something something:' I thought it was a bit inappropriate. I wasn't really looking for that. Your skin wasn't like anything I had ever felt before. It felt like rubber.

You sent me a message: 'I think you have a beautiful nose...
I'd never hurt u even if we fell out.'

Do you remember how 'Fluffy' came in at night and crept up on the bed to lick between our toes? I'm sorry to hear Ginger got run over.

Cauldron of the coming-back

You take a drink,
But only if you're dead,
You make a wish,
But only if you're mad.

There is a thirst,
Which only phantoms know,
Revive my love,
 If that's the way to go.

There is a place,
Upon your clear white breast,
There is a kiss,
Which troopers ought to bless.

If I return,
If lovers come again,
A whole new world,
I carry for all time.

You made me a fish curry which was actually very nice even though you refused to believe it, but I didn't like you forcing my hand to make you climax. You made it very obvious what you were looking for and I felt it was my responsibility to oblige, but I didn't enjoy any of it. You made me suck your breasts to see if they were still providing milk. Emily was six, so you would have had to be doing something very unusual for them to go on producing for so long. Anyway, I went along with the occasion, but it all seemed a bit crazy. You said that you thought Brian had left you because your tummy was too fat. It wasn't that. You said that you never felt really confident about yourself, so I tried to rebuild your confidence as best I could. You sent me two rather abrupt messages: 'I love you dearly!' AND 'Shall we get married?' ???

Adam's tree

In a corner of the garden,
Beneath the rightful tree,
He's sitting with his album,
 Looking seriously.

It is summer in the city,
But here it's always kind,
Below the swaying branches,
And their canopy of leaves.

Slowly through the pictures,
With a deep and broody frown,
Then suddenly he's smiling,
Sending forth a scream.

I wonder what he's thinking,
As he turns another page,
Holidays at Henfryn,
Or a visit to the Barn...

You can almost hear it breathing,
That old and trusty bench,
Stretching through the shadows,
And holding still the cards.

Supposing that I told you,
There's a lesson for us all;
How families stick together,
And manage through the Fall.

How Adam's tree is shining,
Through the caverns of the dark,
Like a candle in your bedroom,
Or a praying in your heart.

The way it should be done now,
Steadfast, true and firm,
Suddenly he's missing,
But his love is here to stay.

There was nothing I didn't like about you physically, and you did have nice blue eyes, but there was nothing I felt particularly attracted too either. You seemed very fragile. You asked me several times: "do you think you could love me, just a little bit?"
I felt a bit unsure because *I didn't know you.* You seemed alright. I thought you had a lovely home, and it was in a scenic part of the country. You seemed to have all the material things in life but very little direction. You acted 'as muddled as a hen at a foxhunt.' One minute you were a drab housewife, next minute 'Mother Theresa,' and then a 'craving nymphomaniac.' I wasn't sure what I was doing there even or what I really wanted from you, if anything. You said that when you came back from Saudi and were living in London you were quite promiscuous and only used men for sex (but not that many!). I tried to make excuses for your conflicting changes of opinion by saying you were trying to view life from a number of different angles, but I disagreed with you about your priorities and how you conducted your life. I decided you were totally wrong for me, but that it didn't really matter because I was never going to stay with you. I told myself that I should never get involved with you or your family; that they were incongruous and

always bickering. You told me that you had once been into witchcraft, and that you used to read the Tarot cards. We destroyed the pack I had by burning them in the garden shortly after. I never liked them anyway. One day you nearly killed us both. You were driving towards Cowley roundabout and were about to drive out into the oncoming traffic, when you shouted: "Bread!"

Assault of the grimy bone-shaker

She lay half-tipsy on the grass,

Her knees,

Drifting,

Heedlessly apart.

"How on earth?"

I curiously asked.

A glare,

A gaud.

Of hurtful blue-and-white.

There is a reason why I never intended to stay, which I would like to tell you about...You asked me if we got along and I said 'yes'. I decided then that I could always come back to you whatever happened; it was your vulnerability and craziness...your desire, and your gregarious nature. I felt you would always need me. I went to bed with you without any real yearning at all; because you seemed to want me there. You gave me one of Brian's t-shirts to wear. You turned up at my place of work early in the morning and shoved a card through the letterbox. It was pink and very sweet. You woke me up. I had just got Adam out of bed and was making tea.

Putting on Emily's shoes

In the morning, when you rub your eyes,
The door opens, And mummy calls:
"Hurry, or we'll be late!"
Our jeep lies purring in the driveway.

You sit above me on the stairs,
Your brown hair, Straight down by your sides,
You look at me, Without a whisper,
Waiting for something, Eating your biscuits.
I try to comb your strands,
But you shake them again, wilfully.

I hunt for your footwear among the bric-a-brac,
The assortment of toys and boxes…
One push and I'm sure it will be alright,
But your tiny feet seem far too big for the space…

So, I undo your straps and start once more,
In earnest,
Trying to persuade them in,
Coaxing them along,
And tie them gently…
Now you are free to stand,
And I can swing you up,
high into my arms,
My Sweet Emily.

You used to ask me where I was: *all-the-time.* You sometimes pleaded with me to let you drive across and stay the night. You seemed desperate not to be left on your own. When I rang you from work it was quite funny: "two minutes" – you'd disappear, and all I could hear for ages was shouting while you tried to put the kids to bed. You put a lot of pressure on me, which I wasn't really prepared for, but I continued to come round to see you, even though I never felt really sure about my intentions. I am a very quiet person in spite of my outward appearance, and I'm very shy sometimes. I don't like a lot of people around. I find it hard to concentrate.

About three weeks after we had started sleeping together I went to Wales with my employers. You tried to speak to me every single night. Sometimes I didn't even answer. To tell you the truth, I wasn't really interested in you. Rose once said to me that she didn't know how you managed to hold down your job at the Surgery. You were reprimanded for not taking enough time with a patient and for doing your shopping during work time. Rose asked me if you were still drinking and where you were hiding all the bottles. I should have been more understanding. I should have been more sympathetic about what you had been through and the stresses in your life. We both agreed that all we wanted was for you to be happy. I should have been more *loving*. Rose said that she and Dennis had been intervening in your marriage and helping to heal the arguments for the last four years. On the night Brian restrained you and you called the police to have him arrested, he said: "there's no way I'm putting _this_ in _there_!" No wonder he didn't come back for six weeks. You said that the reason your relationship lasted so long was because the sexual side had always worked so well...sharing confidences and making disclosures to each other is very important too. For a long time you hid your married name from me, which was: _'Strange.'_

PIECES OF BURNT ASH

A little angel,

stood blushing at our door today,
Her name was Lydia.

My perfect tin soldier nestled gloriously in her arms,
she carried it home, to her mother.

Pieces of burnt ash,
crumble like Sinners in my hands,
the sweet and soulful letters I had written.

I tried to help you, but I didn't want to touch you. I don't really know why. I am very sensitive to location and to the situation I'm in. I once went through your entire wardrobe and drawers. I read everything I could in an effort to understand where I was. It was in the days you left me at home on my week off.

I never saw you wearing anything sexy or seductive.

I watched you go and pay for the petrol in Benson once and watched you walk back again. I couldn't see a single thing I desired, which is very regrettable. Botched hair-transplants aside. Do you remember the flies that summer? They were everywhere. On the ceiling, in the bedroom, on the fly paper. I cleaned the house several times and hoovered them up in thousands. The local newspaper said it was the farm nearby. Apparently, it was a problem every year.

We went along to church together and I met all your friends, even though I had rejected standard Christianity long ago. Then you said you wouldn't go if I was going. People were asking you why we were living together when we weren't married.

It was a taste of normal family life I had never had. It was sweet to see the children attending their little groups. I suppose it must have happened to me once-upon-a -time. I went to pick you up at a nearby Garden party. I was a bit late. You cried and ran to me. I never saw anyone so pleased to see me.

The *first time* I started to care about you was after seeing you trying to play the violin in church. It was hilarious. Very brave!

I remember you calling a dinner party. You invited a lot of your old friends, including Justine. She told you that she thought I was very well groomed. I wasn't really in the mood for socialising but I tried my best for you. They were all decent professional people from fortunate backgrounds and very respectable. Your behaviour was a bit erratic though. Later in the evening as we were at the table I stood up. It was quite subdued in the candlelight. (I sometimes cooked you a meal, especially if I was off work, for you to come home to). You suddenly threw yourself into my lap and begin crying and kissing my hands. (You have a way of doing this which is quite endearing, but it was too <u>threatening</u> for me). It was one of the most touching things I remember about you.

I told your friends that I was standing by you. I didn't know if I was your therapist, lodger/housekeeper, or lover....

You invited me to Malta very early in our relationship. I was quite flattered, but I didn't really want to go. I believe that quality time is better spent at home. I remember walking out on you three times during our relationship. Once was in Malta. I'd had enough of all the children's crying and their spoilt petulant behaviour.

I *had* been invited on holiday by a work colleague: a big Kenyan girl, who actually asked me through Pam. I got along with her very well, and she definitely liked me, but I went on holiday with you out of a sense of duty, and feeling I was a *member of your family*. I asked her what she thought of you after you had come to our barbecue. She said you were 'very pretty.'

I remember *that* barbecue in the garden very well. You sat down on the grass near the strawberries, with your legs up a little. I was really shocked to see very bad bruising all over your inner thighs high up. When I asked you about it you said that it had been caused by riding your old bicycle through the village. The only other time I have seen bruises like that was with a girl I taught literacy skills to, at the Trust. I saw them one day when I unexpectedly found her sitting in our toilet and wondered if I should report it, because I suspected abuse at her home.

I met your Aunty, and quite a few of your family. I was struggling to find anything to bond me to you though. I kept saying to myself: how often has this happened? You start with no feelings at all, then suddenly they fly in from god knows where. Do you remember going on the giant banana boat in Gozo harbour... and falling off? They did that deliberately to us.

Do you still have the pearl earrings I bought you on holiday?

I would have preferred to go abroad on our own rather than with Roger and his screwball entourage. It could have made a big difference. It might have helped. I left a message for you to read at the top of the apartment. It was hidden inside a jar...

One of the most enjoyable days I ever spent with you was playing at the side of the river in Wallingford, just beyond the bridge. We frolicked for hours with a burst football, throwing it up in the air and catching it. We pretended to push Benji in the river and wouldn't let him get out of the water.
We were larking around there all afternoon.
Do you recall sitting on the high bench in the castle grounds? We often went there at the weekend.

I tried to understand you. I thought that one day my feelings might suddenly grow, but I struggled to find a way to connect to you. I even wondered if you had a soul. You seemed to be so disconnected. Then I found your bottle of 'Prozac.'
I think it's a mistake to think that people have to be very alike to get along though.
It may have been my intuition telling me something. From the moment I first drove up to your front door I kept telling myself; if this goes wrong you could end up in serious trouble or you could even die.
I never really committed myself fully to you. I am extremely sorry for being so disingenuous. You must have been very confused.
You once said to me; "You don't come here for sex, so what do you come here for.... I don't do a single thing for you, do I? I can feel it."

Trying to say goodbye

On Thursday, I will try to say goodbye,

I will leave you, and go away...

Forgive me, If I leave a few words scattered around the place,

Behind my painting hung up next to the fish tank,

At the back of the drawer,

Or hidden in your handbag...

If I kiss you all goodnight,

As I softly close the door,

And hold your hand before I go.

Brought along in handcuffs

I was seated in my chair,
Under the yellow spotlight,
Listening to their stares,
Keeping an eye on their voices,
With the tape-recorder running,
And interrogated about *chocolate*,
About the *Quality Street*,
Found in her coat pocket,
Which she'd handed round to friends.

'There were even more liars on the
inside, than there were on the outside'

I didn't like drinking wine every night, although I often went out
to that off-licence in town. They must have got sick of seeing me I
went there so many times for you in the evening. Wine gives me a
headache. I could quite happily go the rest of my life without a
drink. My dad had a bad drink problem and I never wanted to
be like him. I used to check your phone sometimes, and all it had on
it were messages from me, or occasionally, Penny…You said you
had fallen out with her, and then I would find you both drinking
together in the garden.

I am sorry for using the 'thing' with you. How did I ever sink to
that? Some people might see the funny side, but it should never be a
substitute for normal loving. I saw you sat up in bed looking at it
once. I don't think you really liked it, although you said you knew

someone who would. You stripped off on the sofa to use it once. I used to hide it under the stairs. Then it suddenly disappeared. You thought Rose might have found it. How embarrassing...I suspect it finished in the bin.

You pleaded to stay with me at Grays road one night. The laptop was on my bedside cabinet when we decided to watch a film. When I turned it on the most hard-core porn suddenly started playing. It was a short clip of something which had turned up in my e-mail and I had started watching. I suppose we all get a bit bored sometimes, but I hated to think of you knowing I had watched things like that. I actually don't like porn. I remember you sitting up in the bath at Grays road, and me shampooing and washing your hair. It's a memory which will never fade with the years.

I got to the point where I didn't even want to scratch your back in bed. I used to turn over and sleep at the other side. Sleeping has been a big problem for me for years and I fidget like mad sometimes. I don't find it at all easy to sleep when someone else is there. It probably goes back to my childhood, when me and my sister lay in wait for my father to come home.

I know you were sad and confused by my behaviour. I was very aware of you lying there with your eyelashes fluttering wondering what you should do. I know you wanted to sleep with your head on my chest but it felt too intense. Too much, too soon!

You once called out "Help!" You once crept your hand slowly up my leg. All you wanted was to be close to someone. I am very sorry I found that such a strain. I like privacy and solitude. I even went to sleep in the spare room sometimes, as Brian had done.

You even found me on the floor in the spare shower-room once.

You started to drink more. I went to the house one evening quite late to find you in a terrible state in bed. I can't even describe how bad. I don't think it was at all good for the little ones.

You said: "you're never going to give up your job to be with me!" You asked me about my bank account and how much I was worth.

I did offer to help you pay your mortgage. I did help where I could. One evening you had fallen into a coma. I couldn't wake you and I got very worried. For ages I just sat and talked to you and stroked your hand. I thought that maybe your soul would be listening somewhere. I found it very unsettling and I didn't get any pleasure from being with you. I wasn't comfortable.

That didn't stop me from trying to communicate with you and spreading little tears over your eyelids while you were slumbering. You told me that if I wanted sex I could touch you or do anything to you, even if you were asleep. If I could have found a way to find you more appealing, I would have done. I have to apologise for touching you inappropriately while you were asleep. It wasn't nice, and it wasn't enjoyable. Ok, a little!

While you were asleep on the sofa downstairs once I discovered you were wearing a pair of black knickers with a huge patch in the crutch which had been frayed to almost nothing...

You stopped smoking and <u>then</u> you had a fag in your mouth. I hate to see women smoking. Were you trying to tell me something? You had a hard look on your face, which alarmed me...I don't know where it came from. You even asked if I was 'gay.'

We went out for a meal with Adam at Waterstones.

It was in the middle of the *Michael Jackson* court case.

You sailed off to buy a CD of his smash hits. That night I wondered where you had gone and found you dancing down in the kitchen again.

When I first met Benji he was on his own. I was shocked by how small and young he was. He was only seven or eight. I recall what a sweet little voice he had. I think he knew it too. He would sit beside me while we played on the computer or while watching telly. I couldn't understand how easily he kept beating me at World cup soccer. I saw you watching us through the kitchen window as we played at 'shooting-in' on the lawn.

I wanted to teach him so many things. About empathy and trust. About good manners, respect for others and how to express feelings. I went off to buy him a new football down at the nearby shop because he asked for one.

When I came back he just kicked it in the corner. I suddenly realized he had several footballs there already.

I never saw kids with so many bluddy toys and dolls just lying around. Their bedrooms were full of them and they were always getting more!

His leg went a bit septic once, so I cycled out every day to the chemist to buy him some antiseptic dressings and clean his wound. You wanted me to take him to football practise, which I did. At night he would come and bang on the bedroom door or throw things if he heard a sound. He once attacked me with a plastic sword when I came out. You said he had walked in on you and Brian *making love*. I didn't like the way there was no privacy. There was a lodger, with people coming and going all the time. The atmosphere was bizarre. Something seemed to be missing...

Then I met Emily. A bright funny little girl with lots of character. They reminded me of my sister and me. Both very different but also remarkably similar. The only person who came between *us* was 'Catty.' It was a bluey-grey colour. She called it Catty. It had whiskers. It could have been a mouse. She carried it everywhere and would cry if it wasn't there. Do you remember a *little tin doll* I gave her on her birthday? She burst into tears when she saw it. It was nice. You laughed at her...!

I once brought her some 'rock' back from the seaside. She turned and pranced up the stairs with it in her mouth. What a little show-off. She was definitely a little girl!!!

She still trailed around with her dummy in. She was a bit old for one, but it would have been cruel to take it off her. It suited her. I often read her a bedtime story until she fell asleep. The last story I remember reading to them both was 'the Magician's Nephew' which was one of my old favourites. I'm sorry I never managed to finish it. Roald Dahl's Big Friendly Giant was another one. I read it to them more than once. You told Penny we were finished, and then she saw us together at the pool.

I remember swinging Emily round in the garden by her ankles and throwing her up high into the air in the swimming pool at the Phoenicia in Valetta. She reminded me of myself in some ways. The children never seemed to have a proper breakfast. Everything seemed to be done in a panic.

I remember putting on her shoes halfway down the stairs one morning....

We were coming back from the fish shop in Wallingford one night. Her tiny little frame was perched in the passenger seat of my Mitsubishi Warrior. I thought it would make a good family car. I remember going to buy it with you.

She suddenly said; "Andrew. Who do you love most. Me or mummy?"

I thought for a while. We weren't getting along too well by this stage, even though I still did my weights and sunbathed in the garden every day...perfection at all costs!

"I love you both the same but in different ways," I eventually said. And I always will no matter where she is or how big she gets.

We went to a ballet concert, the first I had ever been to, at the little theatre in Wallingford. You were acting weirdly for some strange reason. If we had been really getting along I would have held your hand all through the performance. It was your behaviour which put me off you. For an intelligent woman you seemed to be so shallow and fickle. Emily sat on my knee as usual. I wish I could have hugged her more, but she would probably have squirmed and tried to get away.

I leant forward and kissed her little head. You were there. Some of her hairs got stuck to my mouth. She always smelt nice.

She sometimes cheated at cards. I think you should have told her not to do that. She once pretended to comb my hair....so she obviously had a great sense of humour.

She had a little pound money container. I didn't like you to encourage it, but I didn't have the heart to discourage it either. Reluctantly I made a donation.

After Emily realised Benji could get away with staying in our bed at night she thought she could too. In the end we all slept together in a heap. I think it's called 'pigging.' It bonded me a lot with you all, and it made me feel left out when I came in at night later and saw you all together.

Whenever I could I always kissed you all before I left. I was always happy for them to be there and I never wanted to push them away or take them anywhere else except their own home.

I don't think it did anything for our love-life, but it did bring us closer together. It gave me a break from the pressure of trying to satisfy you. Who knows. It might have happened naturally one day.

I admit that I have had my problems...

"Are you going to be my new daddy now?" asked Emily.

There isn't anything I wouldn't have done to protect and guard them both from harm. If Emily had been mine I don't think I could ever have left her, and I would have taken her round with me everywhere I went. When you first introduced us, she was standing through the door in the lounge. I felt an immediate bond. She took my hand and dragged me around with her for weeks. No matter how much I loved her, I could never have loved one more than the other. I will never forgive you for turning them both against me and robbing me of their most precious years.

Little Wing

The blackened branch,
on which he sang,
so sweetly,
at my side.

But as the morning,
from the land of Giants,
I awoke.

Carried him,
so tenderly,
to the garden, in my arms.

You might think that what happened before we met was not important.

You might wonder why I have to mention these things now, but I do...!

I met a wonderful attractive lady with reddish brown hair called Mary Holmes (I knew her first as 'Lizzie'). She is the reason why they found the things they did.

She was intelligent as well as very beautiful. Some people just have it. Whatever 'that' is. When I went to meet her I always felt happy. A nightingale sung in my heart.

When she nestled her head in my lap, just like she used to do with her dad, and I put my arms around her with my head on hers it felt lovely. It felt like *TRUE LOVE*.

One word, one message from her and my heart seemed to soar into paradise. She didn't like men who tried to hide their baldness.

I only went with her three times, and even then, I was getting migraines. I drove halfway across the country to see her and all the time it felt natural.

Even if she was asleep she could hear me speaking and would answer me. The problem was: every man who met her seemed to feel the same way.

She was tall: nearly six foot.

She told me that I was a really nice guy, but that she needed someone to make her feel small. To be honest I do like tall women, but I hate having to stand on tip-toe or having to walk on the upside of the road. I was devastated and fell very ill. My face actually started to swell up.

She'd been married to a six-foot five *black* American basketball player. Her parents had begged her not to marry him, but she said he was unbeatable in bed.

She said that marrying him was the worst mistake of her life, yet she said that it would not put her off going with another one. I decided that it was the final straw. I would do a couple more paintings and make one final collection of poems before ending it all. I still needed to find a way. Then I met you....

I came over to work in Oxford after being offered a very lucrative job with a reputable academic family close by. It also meant that my then girlfriend could visit me more easily. She lived near Coventry and was a Probation Officer. She was very pretty with blonde hair and big blue eyes. We were perfect in every way except one. She was very sociable and relaxed, while I am a hermit who prefers to live in dark mysterious caves. If only I'd met her sooner.
I am very confident, but I'm also a great perfectionist.
We first met on the train to Oxford, and walked around hand in hand all day. She was a really lovely person, and there was certainly some good chemistry, but even with her I was a complete idiot sometimes and couldn't act *normally*. She
put up with me for a long time though. I think she really cared for me and she didn't want to hurt me. After we went to Florence together I checked her e-mail and realized she had been with an ex-boyfriend just after we had a slight tiff, a week before.
Unbeknown to me he had been pestering her for months.
I just knew something was wrong: apart from me I mean. We were about to take a bus trip around Florence and we climbed on board. She sat half-way down the bus. I walked all the way down to the back. She started crying....
I carried her little picture around in my pocket and slept with it under my pillow for over a year...
I was five years old when I first saw Lydia. She had just started school. I remember her being brought into our classroom and blushing near the door just as I had done. I loved her all the way

through school. When I was eleven my mum and dad were going through a very unhappy divorce. My dad used to get very violent when he had been drinking, and a lot of it was directed against me. We were in the top class, and due to leave. We were due to go to different schools. I remember agonising for months how to tell her how I felt, but never did, even though I saw her looking at me sometimes. I found it easy to tell my mum when I *sat on her knee!* I was sixteen when I saw Lydia walking with her sister down the street. She lived on the next street to my uncle and grandmother. Everyone could see that she was pregnant.

I knew from that day that I could never ever be happy.

When I was forty-three, someone sent me some details from a dating agency. I rang the owner and managed to get her phone number. The woman who answered could have been my Lydia. She talked about her family having to flee Eastern Europe at the beginning of the last war.

I wrote a long letter to her, and only at the end did I tell her about the girl I used to know. I was working down in Kent at the time. She rang my mum wanting to speak to me. She wrote a very sincere and heartrending letter all about her life.

She spoke about a toy soldier I had given to her in the school playground when I was eight. It had been very important to me but I had forgotten all about it. She also brought back other memories I had forgotten (and I thought I had a good memory). She spoke about a shy little boy at school, who was like her in every way.

She said: "Andrew, we all have problems, just different ones!"

"The soul is immortal, and lives far beyond this space and time."

She said: "this is the love I would have always wanted…"

I found her very deep and moody though. She warned me about how hurtful she could be…Lydia was still living with someone in a large house on the outskirts of my home-town, but they were getting divorced she told me. She would ring me in the middle of the night and beg me to take her away. I went to bed with her several times but I just couldn't find any desire. When I couldn't, or wouldn't, make love to her, she burnt all my letters and sent them back to me in the post...

When I opened her letter, I could feel my heart stop beating. I nearly fainted.

That's the first time I ever thought about ending my life.

You once said that you had done when Brian left.

As you know, I once worked for *the Samaritans*.

I managed to persuade a gangster in Chicago to send me a revolver disguised as automobile parts. I told him it wasn't to hurt anyone else, but that I knew someone who wanted to end their own life. It was nothing to do with me hurting any other person: it was about being a failure and worrying about growing old. Too many things had gone wrong to mention. I was close to someone in my early twenties, but lost her. He said he would send me ten bullets to practise with. I had no idea what dum-dum bullets were or how to fire a gun. I wasn't even sure what a firing pin was. I'd never seen one before. The Owner said that he didn't know if it would be any good to me...I tried to contact him again because it kept falling apart and seemed to be welded in the middle but his phone didn't answer. It had a swastika on the barrel, and appeared to be from the First World War, a Browning revolver, with 'museum de Belgique' stencilled on it...I was scared to go near it and kept moving it from place to place. I told myself that I would not change my mind. That was when I met you. The gun was nothing to do with you. It was a silly idea: although we all have to die some day, and I would rather it was quick. My stepfather was dying of cancer and has now passed away. I should have thrown it away or just talked to someone about how I was feeling. You knew something was wrong but I didn't think you would be able to cope with what I told you. Quite understandably you would have been very worried about me. I bottled it all up every night, and that is why I behaved like I did.

That is why, even when you were doing your best to love me, even when you were following me from room to room all weekend, so I didn't abuse myself, flooding me with affection, I couldn't open up and say anything.

I must say I have always been a bit of clown. I have played a number of practical jokes over the years, but nothing as bad or as serious as the ones which followed.

Benji had gone to his friends in Eyam when I decided to close the cottage I had been renting in Wymondham. It was costing me a fortune, and I was hardly ever there. We went across to pick up all my things with Emily. You made me call at my mum's, but they were out. I wonder if that would have changed anything?

I really regretted Benji not being there. My mum would have loved him. She would have really spoiled him. I greatly regret him missing her, because I think he would have loved it too. My mum has a great way with children.

I remember getting some fresh prawns and going down to the beach in Sheringham. You were really annoying me and I was ready to finish with you when we got back. I suppose I must have appeared very grumpy and bad tempered. I was suffering from insomnia and I felt unhappy and under a lot of pressure.

Emily changed on the beach and went to splash in the sea. She was very funny and loved every minute of it. I went in as well.

I got some paint things out at the house to give her something to do. I still have a painting she did.

I am really sorry I couldn't be more normal with you. I am really sorry I worried you. I was horrible to you, and you didn't really deserve it. You were still very loving. Still trying to help me. Your attitude was strange. I didn't feel any connection with you and your ways. You once said that you were even more sensitive than me. I drove back as quickly as I could. When we got near home you said: "Can't you drive any faster?"

I told you that you should be more loyal to people. I am sorry I ignored you for most of the journey.

When I returned to Grays road you sent me a message to say you didn't want to see me anymore. I couldn't have blamed you, but after all the attention you'd given me, if anyone was going to finish with someone, it was going to be me!

I called round to see Rose and Dennis. I couldn't believe it when he told me to go away or he would call the police. I thought he was being a very horrid little man. After all the times I had spent at his home. When I eventually found you, we made up and I stayed the night again. I might have been a lot closer to you than I thought. I helped you with some repairs and did all sorts of chores which needed doing around the house. You said that Brian had never bothered. I finished taking the 'willy-pills' you had bought.

Property

When we returned from Norfolk I put some of my possessions into the garage, and a few in the house. These included:

☐ A brand new large screen TV
☐ Some of my favourite DVD's: *Spiderman* and *Excalibur.*
☐ A brand new hi-fi (which resided under the fish tank)
☐ A new DVD recorder given to me by *Leonard Cohen.*
☐ A brand new mountain bike for you to use in place of your old one (we went out sometimes at the weekend in an effort to get you fitter or did some running on the hill)
☐ A new web-cam/I stocked your book-shelves with the Classics.
☐ I left some of my best CD's in your stack and I bought you some new ones: *Wishbone Ash, Best of Taste, Jethro Tull* and *Cream.*

I did a small watercolour which you hung above the fish tank...I stuck a note behind it:- 'you gave me a dream of a happy home and family, something I never really had, and I gave you this little picture, which I mistakenly thought would be my last'
I left a large picture of you in the garage. I think I had your face

perfect at one point, but I took it a bit too far as usual...

I left you a selection of books, including *'Understand your mind.'*

In one of the books I wrote - 'for Benji and Emily - I love you both....'

Car boot sales

We did a few car boot sales together, mainly at the Kassam.

Do you remember me in the back of the pick-up giving away almost everything I owned for next to nothing? Bottles of wine, mini TVs - everything. I sold a lot of other things when you weren't there. You went off to get some drinks and a bacon sandwich for me with the kids. I think some items were stolen because I couldn't keep my eyes on everyone. You looked puzzled and a little confused. You kept wondering why I was giving away all my worldly goods: well now you know...! You told the fuzz I had sold everything I had at the sales.

You even betrayed me with your neighbours.

That dog of theirs was like Sherlock bloody Holmes; always picking up my scent.

<u>Internet dating</u>

I had relationships with a lot of different women from all around the world while living in Oxford. I saw the way people went from one partner to another, and I never wanted you to do the same. It seemed such a waste of time and effort. I think the best relationships develop and deepen over time.

You told me you had met two other people between Brian and me. One was a vicar with funny shoes, and the other one worked in a supermarket at Didcot (I found a message from him saying he had to go home but that he didn't want to). You told me you didn't want to see him but he kept pestering you? I couldn't understand why you were so ashamed to tell your friends how we had met.

Just before you, I met Honor. She mixed with some of the Royal family and her parents owned land all over the place, with a restaurant in Italy. I'd seen it all before we met. She was very into exhibitionism, which I really wasn't. She brought a lot of presents when she came over including some Italian wine and some cheeses from Perugia. She gave me a little handmade bible which she had been given in Mexico. She had written 'I love you' inside.

Honor was very bright and sensual, but we were like chalk and cheese x

`````````````````````````````````````````````````````````
```````````` .

When I returned to *Robert Sparrow Gardens* one day you told me you had been with three different men that week while I was away. *You told me that you wished the sexual side had worked better in our relationship because it would have brought us a lot closer together.* When I checked your phone and e-mail it appeared to be true. One of the messages said; 'right thing wrong time, I enjoyed it too!'

You said that you had only just met one of them on the street. I was under a lot of pressure at the time. I would like to tell you why. I still didn't want to touch you. You told me that you wouldn't be bothered if you went with five different men in a week. Before this incident happened there had been only me.

You told me one of them was only interested in 'sex.'

You said that you wouldn't mind using the internet for sex.

I told you I didn't want to lose you.

I didn't know what to say or what to believe.

You said I already had.
I saw your eyes water when you looked at me.


You said you were going to marry someone called Dave.
You said you could feel it.
I said, "but you haven't even met him yet...!"
It was all very puzzling. I didn't know what to do.
Then you told me that you thought you might have dreamt it all...
I had wondered about some kind of threesome to get me interested. I once left Rachel a note near the washing machine one night. She sometimes came down to unlock the door for me. It was very brazen. You were snoring away upstairs. I asked her if she wouldn't mind coming and sucking on your breasts for half an hour...I couldn't believe it when she thought for a while, and then said ..." Oh, alright!" She was the nurse from Nigeria.
I didn't take her up on it and left soon after, but your voice sounded a bit quaky when I spoke to you on the phone the next day.
I came back one night and you told me to go away or you would call the police. I had a key cut when you left me to go off to work. When I went back the next night you asked me if I would be staying all week.
You were in a terrible state. I had a pretty good idea you had been with someone. I still felt nothing except bewilderment: no feelings. I told you that you didn't have to behave like that.
You were lying in Emily's bed when we started petting.
You told me David had brought an overnight bag the first time you met. You went to pick him up at Cholsey station. I've hated the place ever since. The men you went with all seemed to fizzle out. You told me that you might have sex with me next, or it could be someone else. I thought your behaviour just wasn't right.
Your tongue was wagging about as I looked down on you in the light from the doorway.
"If you could make love with anyone in the whole world who would

it be?" I asked. You hesitated a second and said..."You?!"
What can I say?
Your craziness was exasperating. Perhaps I had started to care
about you. It's the one thing I do miss a bit.
The love I had only felt in your hands started to come back again.
Perhaps you are a *Healer* like me...?
I woke up one night with you feeling the top of my head. You shot
your hand back. Bound to be curious I guess. I wasn't angry. It
was quite sweet. Then one night your arm suddenly flopped over
me. You laughed when I made a funny sound in bed.
We started having sex during one of your periods and I got your
blood all over me...another time I found you wearing knickers in
bed. You asked me if I would be taking my things when I went.
I left them there because I always thought I would come back...
And I never wanted you to forget me.

A pair of socks you gave me to wear!

## AN INCIDENT

In August something really ghastly happened. You kept asking
me what was wrong.  You said there was something wrong. You
told me about a dream you'd had: *You'd gone somewhere to see me.*
*Some of your friends were there. The flatfoots were there too, but*
*they wouldn't let you into the building.* It was a stupid petty little
business, which was blown right-out-of-proportion. I was
struggling to know what to do with you.  I was bored and fed-up.
My life just didn't feel at all happy, and I wasn't cut out for

31

balloon dancing. I didn't do anything sexual. I suppose I just like to shock people sometimes. I really should know better. It was a very silly thing to happen. All it brought me was misery. I told you that I'd had an argument with someone in town. I was very ashamed of letting you down.

I called in a shop on the crowded High street and started trying on clothes. One of the Assistants came back with a pair of trousers. When she handed them over through the changing room curtain she saw that I was only half dressed, and that was all. She turned and walked away without reacting. Two to three seconds at most. The Assistants could be seen acting out what had happened on the shop video. I walked calmly out of the door.

No matter what you think about these things, it certainly doesn't deserve the title 'Sex-offender,' and I did not deserve the awful repercussions which followed.  Nor was I going to attack anyone, or wait for someone after work!

It wasn't something I could really talk to you about even though you ran a clinic on sexual health.

The Authorities must have known about me and you. I am surprised they didn't come rushing round to tell you bad things about me then...? Shortly after it happened you were leaving work when the miserable toads fined you for not wearing your seat belt. About three weeks after the original incident I cycled into town down Headington hill and saw there were people in plain clothes and uniforms scattered in every nook and cranny along the route. When I came out of 'Boots the chemist' four officers jumped me and dragged me in handcuffs through the crowded streets to the main police station. I decided to plead guilty to exposure and wrote the Manager of the shop a letter of apology. I just couldn't face a lengthy court case. I was held for ten hours in a police cell while they played their pathetic games.

Poor Adam was at home wandering what had happened to me.

I spoke to Pam on the phone about the appalling situation. She was very understanding. I sent her a text from the police cell saying that 'no-one loved me.' She said that lots of people did.

Pam said I ought to tell you myself what had happened rather than you hear it from someone else. We weren't getting along too well. Even if it had been months earlier I would have found it hard to tell you. You had just started your course at the college.

I needn't remind you that it was my idea you did Osteopathy. You weren't at all happy in your job. I suggested it because I had a friend called Clare Farleigh who had gone on to do it after nursing too. I came up to see you. You were parked outside. You drove off. You said that love had to come from both sides. What a bluddy cheek! You'd started asking me if we were better just being friends. I recall going up the hill to the garden centre. What a cold mood you were in. I was really fed up with you.

I was there one evening around October when you said you were expecting an important phone call or two. You had been away all weekend and your phone was switched off.

When I turned up and asked you where you had been you asked me what I was doing there. You flinched when I touched you. The first time I felt a twinge of desire you pushed me away.

You said you had stayed one night with Karen, and one night with your brother's friend. His wife didn't really like you staying. He was black I think. You said he had been suspended from his job in the Health service for a suspected sexual assault.

You said he once made a pass at you.

You told me your breasts were sore because I had sucked them too hard. When the phone rang you closed the door.

I sat on the sofa in the lounge and tried to hear what you were saying. It all sounded very deep and emotional. Your voice went quite high some of the time.

You kept repeating: "We are friends, aren't we?...you are the best friend I have ever had."

"Friends, yes! Yes, I know you are having trouble with you wife..."

You looked quite secretive and cold when you returned.

Pam once asked me why I always seemed to meet such needy women.

Some weeks I had deliberately stayed away or drove off somewhere else. I am a strange man sometimes I know. I re-united with an old girlfriend down in Maidenhead... I had a special cake baked for your birthday, and I *made you a card* with a poem I'd written inside, just for you. I also ordered you a large bouquet of flowers in Wallingford. I went out to Woodstock shopping for you and found a brown fur-jacket top. I bought you a size too small.

She said I could bring it back if it was too small.

All these gifts I presented to you on your birthday.

I just turned up at the house like before.

You said that Penny had invited you out but that you would rather stop in with me. You wore your new top, even though it was a bit of a squash. I am so sorry for that. I never got chance to change it for the right size. I never got to taste any of that lovely cake either...

On Sunday you invited me to help you at Emily's birthday party in the School Hall. Dennis was surprised to see me. We made friends. He'd had a lot of trouble with his eyes I think...

I helped to pay for the venue as you didn't have enough money. It was a nice day and I remember us taking pictures of Emily running across the floor. She was in her element. I felt very tense. You pushed me away when I touched you which wasn't very nice and you made fun of me. Rose noticed how you were treating me. The Clown-hired-for-the-occasion said he thought I was *with 'Rose.'* Not very complimentary, but you did say Brian had a nice face.

That night I read Benji his story in bed as usual, but I had a splitting headache. You asked me if I would be staying, but I had to get away to my own bed. In the morning I appeared in Court all by myself. I did my best, but still received a hefty fine.

What was even worse: they put me on the Sex offender's register for five years. It meant that the police would be calling round and interfering in my life all the time. I also had the Probation department ringing my employers and trying to cause trouble.

I had just got back from Court when I received a text message from you. I needed all the help I could get. I have never been sure to this day whether the police came to see you and tried to say the most nasty and unpleasant things about me.

Your text message said:

'I don't want to see you again. No further contact.'

My care of Adam was affected by what was going on and I greatly regret that. I think that if he had ever seen you again he would have run you down in his wheel chair. Adam never knew about the Court case. He would have been too upset, so we agreed not to tell him.

I still called round to the house as you know. I didn't know what to say to you so I just stood on the road in the distance.

I sent you a text message. I was used to you *being there.*

You replied with the only truly hurtful message I ever received from you; 'I don't know you!'

That is so true really. I never let you get to know me because I was never sure about you or the future.

I felt guilty that you had known me for eight months, during which time we had slept together on and off, and I had never let you into my heart or confided in you about anything which really mattered or which had altered my life...

I cycled all the way from Oxford just to look in the drive. I even saw Benji and Emily taking Fluffy out for a walk one morning, but I couldn't go near you...!

On one occasion Benji came running from his friends to talk to me. He thought I was coming in, but I told him to go back.

Another time he actually blushed.

There was an occasion a few months later when you had a college teacher with you all morning: a Friday I think.

Benji: "I've just seen Andrew!"

You: silence.... then "Where was he?"

Benji: "Just outside..."

After your friend had gone...

You: "Did you really see Andrew? What did he do?"

Benji: "He just went away!"

You: "Don't talk to him!"

Benji: "Why not?"

"Why do you think...!?" you snapped.

*You might wonder how I know all this...?*

I looked at you one day, and decided you would be the wrong person to joke with.  I didn't think you would ever appreciate a wind-up.

You *said* I would see a different side to you.

You were in the kitchen with Sandra.

Let me tell you something about Sandra. I don't think she's had it as easy as you might think. You were always sensitive about her.

I could see how beautiful she was, but there is no way I could ever have touched her instead of you.

I sent you a message about wizards. It was only meant as a piece of light-hearted banter.

You replied (with Sandra): 'go and see a doctor. You are sick!'

And 'fuk off you <u>impotent loser</u>!'

If you thought things like that would hurt me you are very much mistaken, but you obviously thought they would hit me where it hurt. I thought they were very childish and petty comments to make, and they say a lot about the kind of person you are.

I was shocked that you could send messages like that to me though.

By the way. I never sent you twenty messages a day. You were lucky if you got one or two. I often ignored your messages and never even replied to most of them! I once rode past you on the field. It was at a summer fete close by. You were standing with your arms round Emily...I bumped along over the grass on my bike.

<u>The reasons I came back and what I did there</u>:

I came back because, strangely enough, I actually missed you, and it felt like home...I had often returned to Oxford in the middle of the night to get some sleep.

One day you pulled up right next to me in the car, at the traffic lights in Wallingford. Emily stared at me through the window and seemed very puzzled. I was staying in the George Hotel at great expense and attending the local gym. One of my pictures raised £200 for a lady's cancer charity on the main road.

You were on the computer with them one night. You talked to them about the *devil's number*. You had obviously discussed it with them before because I heard Benji say "666!"

I wonder what they will think of you when they get older?

I sent you a message about once a month, but each time I did I was

there            watching you in the garden...

Maybe I just like spying on people. It's a good way of finding out people's little secrets. I once worked for a Private Detective Agency. It was a teeny bit creepy! But then, the Cops do it all the time. I wanted to see your reaction, to study you like never before. I actually learnt a lot more about you during this time.

You once tracked down your ex all the way to Spain (the German guy who you met as *his* nurse in hospital) and *'groped his partner.'* You said there was *nothing there* (she was "as flat as a pancake!"). So, you know all about this kind of behaviour? You once asked: "You wouldn't ever hurt me if we fell out, would you? I would never hurt you, even if we fell out..."

What a silly thing to say! It was almost as daft as asking me if I would touch Benji or Emily and if I was being friendly to you in order to get to them. I hate that sort of thing. Not in a million bluddy years! I could never have hurt any of you!

I thought it was stupid and insulting.

I saw you next in the Thai restaurant we used to go to, with Mat R. He didn't take his glasses off once, even when you massaged his back on the sofa back home. You kept referring to *me* as 'the nutter.' Thanks!

I saw you take out the photograph album when he had given your chest a really rough kneading under your top. You touched his leg. I watched for a few moments. It was so boring. I felt a bit sorry for both of you and went home.

You left his address, written down, at the side of the sofa. He *used* you *just for the night* and you probably did likewise.

I communicated with him disguised as another woman on-line. He bragged about fking you listening to the BG's on *my* hifi.

I woke about ten the following morning, with a horrible impression. I could feel and hear what you were doing. It was truly awful. I could hear you crying 'ouch...' he *bragged* about having a...l intercourse with you. What on earth were you doing letting a creep like him do that to you!? I could hear a lot of panting and grunting. What a seedy despicable world we live in!

He didn't come back. He must have been quite sane after all.

The next time I saw you, after Christmas, you looked awful...your hair was very bedraggled and you looked pale and drawn. You looked very upset and unwell.  It may have been me. You reported me for leaving some poetry in a drawer, and a Christmas card on the wall...Fluffy always found me, even in the dark.

I was out in the garden when I sent you one of my rare messages. I was watching you carefully, but I couldn't go across or do anything.  The paper with Mat's address and telephone number was still lying at the side of the couch months later.

I texted you: 'I miss u' - that was all.

I saw you read it and nod your head. You started weeping and touched your face. I am so sorry for any pain I have caused you....

I left you a bottle of wine sometimes and other things as well. I wrote a note on the back of my kitchen board until you took it down.  It was the one with a *duck* on the front, which had hung on *my* kitchen wall for years.

I thought it was especially funny to write notes in your Calendar, like 'apologise to Andrew'... (in December).

I am a very sentimental person really. I thought that one day you would understand me better.

A WPC I met at a party in Southampton advised me not to have anything more to do with you. She warned me you were trouble and to keep away from you. She said that *you* were the one with the problem.  Her name was Dee. She wanted a relationship but I didn't.

I remember Howard insisting: "She's reported you once. She'll do it again!"  He was Director of Forestry at Brookes.

Adam's father was getting increasingly exasperated by the police constantly calling at my place of work. He was furious with my antics.  You once sat in his arm-chair by mistake.  He could be quite materialistic but also very kind.

I deliberately set you up with a black guy called Massi, to see how you would react. It was another very silly thing to do. I gave him your name on 'lovenfriends.' He was nasty piece of work. He went around seducing white women on line and then he would display the pictures he took, so everyone could see what he had done with them. I used to read your e-mails between each other. He contacted you under two different names. In one he pretended to be white. He deliberately played mind games with you, so you would choose him. The last I knew he was living in Croydon. I once rang him to find out if you had actually met, but he was very slippery. Not even my Private detective friend in Yorkshire could get any dirt out of him. His usual voice-mail message said: "life is a box of chocolates. You never know what you are going to find...."

I put a photo of you up on line a few months later. He obviously recognised you, and seemed to know a lot about you. He said he wanted to meet someone who was passionate, very sexual, and could keep a secret. He also said he was into Dildos and oral sex. He told me that he had never visited Oxford...

You told him that I had put a picture which looked like you on-line...{A man listed as living at your address, but also with a business address in Oxford, called Calvin Shields, sold marital aids and sex aids on the Internet).

You told a policewoman who called at my place of work that I had put your details on line, because someone told you.

One evening before you met 'Kevin,' you dressed yourself completely in black, with little ringlets in your hair I had never seen before, and you were gone all night.

You looked a bit the worse for wear the next day, but not as bad as before. Your hair looked a bit matted.

In 2006 you sent me a sexually explicit voice-mail message when you thought it was Massi who had texted you. You said that you had once had an incredible sexual experience in your car and that you hoped he would respond. I think you were a bit drunk to be honest. There's a turn up *for the book!*

I am sorry for playing these silly tricks with you. It would take a lot of explaining...I was very unhappy when I saw you meeting regularly with Kevin Br. Naturally, I read all your messages. It lasted a lot longer than I thought it would. I saw Roger in Wallingford. He told me that Kevin was alright, but that he wasn't used to dealing with children. I was there the first night you introduced him to the kids. You kept going back to see how they were getting on. I heard you telling someone on the phone that all Kevin did was stuff himself with cream cakes all day long and talk about his ex-wife. You told them that he certainly wasn't the one for you. You actually described him as 'sweet!'

I went in once when he had hurt his foot and couldn't visit you that weekend. He preferred to go out with 'the boys' anyway, he said. You were in a poorly state in the small room at the front. You had made it into a little bedroom. I felt nothing but pity for you, and went close to you a few times but was frightened to wake you up. I wasn't sure how you would react. You seemed so lonely and alone.

I hated you making fun of me with the kids and their friends.

I hated you playing games at the window and kissing him when you thought I was outside.

I hated seeing his car there, seeing him pawing at your chest, attempting to kiss you, wiping his saliva away, lying on his chest, slopping wine. I wanted it to end.... I knew it would. I thought that I would forgive you though.


I found Massimo's details on your phone when I came in one night. You saw me once in the garden, I think, I don't know how. You went on the phone. I was questioned by a panda car which suddenly appeared from nowhere on the High street.

I returned to the house and saw you were absolutely paralytic. You were on the sofa all alone and looking very unhappy.

I looked at you and said out loud from the garden: "I love you!"

It was as if you could hear me...!

The reaction from you was very upsetting.

You burst into tears like I had never seen before. They were rolling in big lumps down your cheeks and you were sobbing. You started nodding your head exactly as I said it. Could it be that we were linked in some inexplicable and mystifying way?

You got up after a while but you were very rocky and fell, breaking a glass. Fluffy was petrified. He hissed and ran into the corner of the room. As you lay on the floor he was meowing loudly in consternation. I let myself in and cleaned up the glass, then I lifted you up onto the sofa and covered you with a blanket, and then left. I think Kevin had gone to bed to sleep off the booze.

I was there the first night that Yas stayed. I thought he looked Chinese. He kept dusting the side of the sofa. You were upstairs, and when you came down you had a lot of eye makeup on. You kept licking your lips. He had gone upstairs by then. He seemed a pleasant enough fellow. He told you that relationships were never equal. He said that Kevin looked like a *used car salesman*. Yas was always looking for more from you. Originally you told him: "friends, just friends, yes?!"

Yas started coming across on a Friday at a time when Kevin wasn't coming as often. I heard you in the garden begging Kevin not to go, just as you had done with me.

He visited you for the last time at Christmas. You flung your arms round him and kissed him at the doorstep as soon as he came in.

I came back to see Fluffy, sit him on my lap, talk to him, feed him, and clean his tray, which was really disgusting sometimes.

I mended your door which was sticking.

I checked *my property* and your phone. You left your mobile out in the garden more than once.

I put the boot down on your car because you had left it open all night and it was blowing in the wind.

I took some milk to make a drink. Fluffy ran to me when I came. I used to come in late at night and look at you in bed with Benji and Emily holding you on either side. I turned the light off once and you woke up. You must have known it was me. You told Anna: "It's my Stalker. He comes in at night, but I don't think he's dangerous." She was on the Osteopathy course with you.

I left some chocolates in your coat pockets (which I believe you handed round to friends) – the Cops came to interview me about them as you know, because Debbie G. showed you my book. Haven't you ever see the advert...Cadbury's milk-tray? I didn't even know it was a crime.

I was in and out like a 'jack-in-a-box' one night. You were lying in bed. The kids should have been there, but I couldn't see them anywhere. You were all alone I think. It was now or never. Christ, did that floor in your bedroom creak. Back and forth like a yo-yo. Eventually I leant over and kissed you ever so lightly on your forehead. You stirred and moaned a little. I was scared what you might do if you saw me. It was the first time I had touched you in months. It was very tender. I turned and walked carefully away...

On your 43rd birthday you must have been out somewhere. You were dozing on the downstairs sofa when I came in. Your face looked a little thinner. I wondered what it had been through since we were friends. I didn't touch you. I just stood there looking. Your dress was rucked up and your nylons all hanging down. I felt very sorry for you. I took some flower petals from my coat pocket and scattered them in your lap. I didn't dare leave any obvious evidence of my visit because I didn't want any more pigs embarrassing me at work.

I left you another bottle of wine.

I took a pair of your used knickers (to my surprise they were very intoxicating) but delivered you *another toy* for under your pillow. I left two little jugs. You kept some papers in one. I heard you say to

Rose: "I don't know where they came from!"
I made them myself in Adam's kiln, at the Barn.
I played tricks on you with the keys. I sometimes took them from
your keyring and had them for *all* the doors. I thought I had lost
the front door key once so went in and took the only one you had. I
am extremely remorseful about that. I heard you outside
trying to get in. You had to go around to Rose's. I heard Benji and
Emily sighing;
<u>"locked out of our own home!"</u>
I left a little bonnet I had bought at the British library for Emily. I
hope she wore it. I left your Christmas presents under the tree.
I checked my note to see if it was still there, and when it wasn't
replaced it with a carbon copy (as you know!).
I wrote in your address book.


I signed you up to an internet telephone account and monitored
your calls.
I twiddled with my thumbs and wondered what to do.
I used the loo, or had a bath.
I read all your post.
I changed some of the labels on your Osteopathy skeleton.
I went to the garage.
I moved your vase. The one you had tried to hide behind when Yas
was there...


I tested your electrics and changed a fuse.
I went through your drawers and checked your wardrobe again.
I left a photo in one of my psychology books.
I asked myself various questions:
Do you think this is bordering on obsession?
What if she finds out...
What is going to happen in the end?
How do you think this is going to impact on the rest of your life?

I just didn't want you to forget me! As if you ever could.

I kept a large notebook of my activities. It was really just a jest. I kept it out of boredom really. I needed something to occupy my mind. I have always liked history.

A chap called Shane rang you. He arranged to meet you while you were out at Mayor Dennis's…he was playing with his train set. Shane came from Mauritius. He told me you were keen on his nationality, but you weren't sure about him being phallically challenged and over fifty. If I remember rightly you said that 'anyone who wasn't married and hadn't had kids by the age of fifty wasn't fit for anything.'

You left his details in the *cat basket*.

Then you met Danny. He was the one with 'piggy-eyes.' You told him about me, and went to the pub up the hill. The one we used to go to on a Sunday. You both stared at the sidewall when you drove in the cul-de-sac. He started groping your chest on the sofa a short time after. Not again I thought. By that time Yas had gone up to bed. You left him in the house by himself. He appeared content to step aside but you could tell what he was thinking and where he wanted it to lead.

You were dressed in your usual red cardigan when you went out with Danny that night, and you had applied a lot of make-up. When you came back your face was very pale and you looked terrible. All your make-up seemed to be gone.

When Danny started groping you again you seemed very nervous, but still flung your head into his lap. It all seemed so unreal. As if you were just acting a part.

Yas went to the upstairs window and looked out into the garden. I thought he might have seen me dashing across the lawn.

You were quiet the next night and sat with your back to the window. You looked a bit self-conscious talking to Yas and Anna. Yas liked it better when it was just you and him. He joked about having to lock his door at night, and paying you in sex instead of

board. You 'glared' into space for a long time when he said that.
"Friends, just friends!" you said. You took it in turns to go on-line.
You told Anna you had spent the last four days together.
You read Yas Kevin's e-mail when he finished with you. Kevin said
he had wanted to finish with you before but he couldn't because
Alex (your new lodger) was there.
I sent you a message about having your back scratched. Yas told
you that you if you scratched someone's back they would have to
do the same for you.
 I recall Yas pretending to expose to you, and playing charades at
the bathroom window.
You told him about the church in London and your friends there.
You bragged to him about being a 'Scorpio.'
That night you sat there applying heavy lipstick and doing your
finger nails. You kept applying lip-gloss, as he sat behind you.... I
couldn't see if he was touching your bra-strap or not.... your eyelids
began flickering nervously, then you looked very worried and self
conscious, then you looked very hard and a bit upset, and got up.
You went back to the computer. He castigated himself, as if he had
missed his chance. You both kept getting up to visit the bathroom.
The next message I sent you was a bit of tease.
I said that you were bound to turn someone on if you had your
breasts sucked by them. Yep, I am a twit!
You told Yas I was your 'Stalker,' and that you couldn't stand me.
I heard you saying the same thing about him on the phone to your
sister a few days later.
You sent me a message with him at your side and asked for his
help. It said;
'squishy little pink dick' and (once more) the well-worn 'fuk off u
impotent loser!'
He was quite submissive most of the time.
I went in one night and heard you open your door and pretend to
scream to see if he would come to your room.

Sandra the Vicar's wife asked you if he *smelled*.
When you showed him a picture of Danny. Not a very attractive
person by all accounts, Yas said, "well, maybe he has a big dick?"
You replied: "I don't like it when you talk like that!"
All this seems so familiar...
You asked him if he found you 'boring.'
You sat there on the couch, almost laughing, playing with your
bra-strap, sneaking a look at his face. You even had Anna in on
the act one night, while I was freezing out in the garden, in the
pouring rain....
I left a poem about Fluffy for Benji. You took it down after a few
weeks. Emily found it and wouldn't go in the Wendy house again.
I never did anything sexual while I was there. I kept my behaviour
impeccable in that respect, the whole time!


I don't know why, but Yas seemed to have decided to keep himself to
himself. You asked him if he would like to go on holiday to Malta:
"I'm on my own and so are you. The kids would love it!"
He asked you to ask him again in the middle of the week when you
were *more sober*.
You wondered if he would like to start a business in Malta...
He said it didn't matter if you were 42-3 and he was 27?
You told him that you couldn't give him any children though...
He suddenly jumped up from our purple sofa and went to bed.
You sat there for ages by yourself, licking your lips and
fantasizing. Putting your hair up, and letting it down again.
Then you fell over, spilling your wine glass.
I don't know what happened when you eventually went up to bed,
but I got bored of sitting around and trying to stand in that little
infant chair to see more.
The next night your face was very flushed as you rushed around
his bedroom, changing the bed sheets...
The next weekend Yas was there with Anna. Benji was on the Osteo

couch. Yas was stroking his head and talking to him the way I used to do. You were a little the worse for wear, but went in the kitchen and started talking to Anna. You told her that he was 'very sexual' and that you had sex with him for hours.

The next night you were alone at your computer touching yourself. A strange thing happened while I was at my caravan round the corner doing your portrait. I put your picture next to a decent picture of me to see what we looked like together. It was very sad to see: we might have been a lot closer than I imagined. I couldn't wait any longer!

I sent what I believed to be my final book of poetry to your father (and I thought you were mad! And you said he was mad!).

As a Professor of Literature, I thought he would preserve my work and when I was dead appreciate my sincerity. Not only did you tell me how your father used to lie down in front of the car to prevent you from attending church, but that he lived with 'Quentin Crisp,' while studying at Oxford. He must have been very gifted to get a Double First. You resembled him in some ways. I suppose it can be very difficult living with someone who has Asperger's?

You were down in Wales with Sandra going through my book the next weekend... ('Small birds sing').

When you came back you took my picture down again because of something I had written inside my book and left the picture on top of the table...I wasn't going to put a message behind it a third time if that's what you were thinking!

I once spoke to your father about the 'Bard.' He was drinking a cup of tea after breakfast on the Living-room sofa. He wanted to know how I could quote from every Shakespearean tragedy. When your parents visited I acted normally and tried to get on with them both. Even though you said your mother was a 'bitch' I was determined to give them a chance and treated them both with respect.

I can get along well with anyone who likes words and literature. I thought you'd inherited other traits from him.

I never noticed your mum's legs. She was quite old. I found her to be more sensitive than you made out.

# Like a prayer-note in the snow

You are there,
I am here,
it's midnight, and...
I drink the starlight.

With eyes like two dark beam-holes in the madness.

The wind burning like irons,
the earth turning like fires.

If only skies had been more unbolted,
if only rain had been more loving.

Your father kept ruffling his head and looking at me. Never seen a bald one before....
I never made a proper effort to dress up smartly and conduct myself in the way I know I can. It was because I had given up on life before we met.
I used to leave my shoes and clothes at the side of the bed. They were always still there the next time I came.
We had a meal with your mum and dad at the table. Sandra was there too. I wanted to talk about religion and politics. Your mum appeared to be a very traditional Catholic and a Monarchist.
I even stood up for your mum a bit when you began putting her down. That is why I was a bit disappointed when you told me she said I "wasn't presentable" - a doctor or a barrister like your brothers. I didn't sell myself or make myself more acceptable. That was my frame of mind at the time. I am very sorry for my faults.

*'Though art a soul in bliss, but I am bound upon a wheel of fire, that mine own tears do scald like molten lead...'*

Your mum said that they had only put up with your ex-husband for *your* sake.

Pam once said of you that I "could do a lot worse...."

When you came back from visiting your mum and dad the police tried to speak to me but I ignored them. I could feel your mother's emotions. She was very upset. She must have read some of my book- it needed additional editing however.
I think she felt disheartened about what was happening.
Adam suddenly died. You remember stopping at his house and meeting his family...? He had suffered a huge aneurism in his head. I was at his bedside holding his big toe when he slipped away.
I brought down all his cuddly toys to put around him at the John Radcliffe: his brown bear, his giraffe, and his blue sea-lion.
I sent you a message from his bedside. His sister was in tears.
You replied: '<u>fuk off, or u r nicked</u>!'

# Garland of seared wood

Motionless you stand,

With a hint of salt,

Like a Sentinel-of-Time, with your felt-tipped sorrows,

Scrolls of spattered paint,

Scratching and piercing the wilderness,

Where a spider's web of colours,

Covers and rambles your nakedness.


Curtseys of brown swooning and swimming the silence,

Unarmed and frail,

Sinking into the earth...


The frost like jewels on a garment of green,

And the hand of the Moon,

like a branch of cinnamon,

Holding you,

Loving you,

The shivers down your spine,

You are really too small for me to rest in.

You were lying on the sofa by yourself. I think you knew I would be round. I just wanted to put my arms round you and make everything alright, but I just couldn't do it. I was scared of someone coming down. The light was on in the bedroom even though it was very late. I went in and out several times, before I suddenly saw Benji at the top of the stairs looking down. He came down a step or two. I would have loved to reassure him, but I simply shut the door and went away. I went back to see him trying desperately to wake you up. His face was pouring with tears, poor lad. What terrible thing had I done to make this happen. What did I ever do to make this poor little boy, who I had carried in my arms to bed each night, so afraid? I suppose I knew it was bound to happen one day, after several close escapes.

You even came down one night in your blue nightie and missed me by a whisker. I nearly tripped over Fluffy on the doorstep.

One time you sat with your head on the kitchen table. I couldn't have done this to anyone else.

Telling them stories, spreading it around that I was a joke. My behaviour was very silly, but I certainly didn't mean any harm. I wouldn't have hurt him for the world or harmed a single hair on his head. I wouldn't have hurt any of you in a thousand million years, but I have been labelled along with the very worse type of people despite my saying this over and over again...

If only we had been able to talk instead of you sending silly messages and shaking your head. You were sitting there one night, all alone and crying. You were wearing a pullover I had given you, which my mum had knitted. I sent you a tease - "that's my mother's woolly pullover you're wearing...!" You nodded emotionally. You felt it's fabric.

It was very touching seeing you in it and it made me cry.

You told Penny about my message...

She replied: 'scary-call the police!'

You told me Penny could be very two-faced.

The next night you locked the front door.
The night after that you didn't.

Crime and Punishment
I had just been to Adam's funeral. There were some lovely people
there. It was all very moving. I'd had my caravan on the site just
round the corner from you for about a year.
Apparently, I *had* been spotted on the road.

# Being a wizard

Being a wizard, as you know,
Gives me the power,
To come and go.

First, you'll see me, Then you won't,
In the sky, Or flying north.

In your dreams I'll sit and talk,
Beside your bed or in your thoughts.
When you wake and take a look,
At the door or in your book.

You'll find me there, Or in the air,
Turned into shade, Or made of wood.
When all the stars come out tonight,
The Moon is bright, For you my love.

You were in the next queue at the supermarket. I tried not to look.
You went back to be with Yas...you told the pigs I had parked my

blue Landrover next to yours and reported me again.

You nearly ran me down on my bike turning in ahead of me the short cut to the Clinic. I volunteered to be a 'guinea-pig' at the centre while you were training in the next room. I asked your colleagues not to tell you... I saw you cycling across the bridge on the old bike, on the other side to me. You didn't even wave.

I went in to see the Vicar of St Peter's to have a chat about us...

The church said I could go in any time...

You reported me for sitting with my bike on the bend.

I am sorry the children were upset and didn't understand.

Eventually I received a 'caution'.

I hated you behaving like a perfect stranger and telling everyone our relationship...

was *never intimate*.

You told them our relationship was never a physical one.

After that night when you lay resting, waiting for me, I went to my caravan. I had finished at Grays road and didn't know what else to do with myself. I was in limbo. The first thing I remember that next morning is the pigs raiding my holiday home and being dragged off to prison. My troubles were only just beginning...

'When I wouldn't give the name of the Senior Probation Officer I'd had a relationship with I was labelled a 'fantasist.'

Every hour in prison was like a living nightmare. It there is a hell on earth its name is 'Bullingdon.' It felt as if I had taken up residence in some kind of mental asylum. Not a hell of fire and warmth but one which was cold and damp, and where time stood still with the passing shadow of the Sun. I grew pale with worry. The walls were whiter still and the fences mounted with 'razor' wire. In-mates were encouraged to take drugs to get through their ordeal. For months I had no-one I could even talk to. A lot of the prisoners had personality disorders or serious learning difficulties.

A lot of guys harmed themselves even without help from the Guards.

# The bellowing of Allan Tom

Ochre was his hated clock,
woad the ridges of his brow,
red the word-way crammed with chalk,
the pest of every classroom.

They waited till the banging up,
dressed in gloves and whites,
they waited till the coast was clear,
guarding his bright doorway.

Into the hell-hole Brownie leapt,
a hit-man, and a Rapist,
smashing Allan's gawping mug,
into a wheelchair gaping.

A sound like wind, a sound so strange,
came blurting from his gully,
spurting from his battered heap,
like a howling genie.

"Who did this to you?" Gaughan asked.
"What a wicked fellow!"
His scarlet face was sheeped in mirth,
 skipping 'long the E-wing...

**'Every time I appeared in court the police added to the number of bullets they found, from a small handful, up to thirty'**

When they charged me with the possession of that old firearm without a licence I was knocked for six. It didn't even work. They charged me with a lesser offence by mistake (Debbie G. was fit though; I nearly kissed her in the Cop-shop). I rang my mum and step-dad. Keith wanted to know what on earth I was doing with a thing like that. I heard the Pigs shot round to tell you the good news. You immediately assumed I was going to kill you. What do you really take me for? The Officers in Bullingdon told me that I would get about eight or nine years in prison. I told my mum that I would rather die...I thought I would die, in prison. At one hearing Judge King tried to give me an 'indeterminate sentence,' for the safety of the general public. The Court hearings went on for months. My name was dragged through all the newspapers. I had to live with the kind of low-life scum I have avoided all my life.

## A natural urge while touching

The way I return to you,

here in this prison cell, Mary.

A microscopic gleam of time,

in Wymondham,

where I was happy.

Like a blissful dolphin, I flew,

jouncing over the waves.

Rarer than foxgloves,

in the depth of winter,

I touched you,

my dear Mary.

I really didn't think I would be able to survive but my friends in Oxford supported me tremendously. They were instrumental in getting me through it and provided the Judge with some very good references. The police tried to paint me in the very worse light possible. The Judge told the Prosecution that they had to stop mentioning the other things they found unless they were going to charge me with them, but they never did. The Prosecution said that there were *many more* charges to come, but nothing more ever materialized. There was a woman in the court who kept smiling at me, who seemed vaguely familiar...

A <u>small amount of cannabis</u> in a bag, with a pipe (I had once experimented with Sarah (the manager of Headington library), who I had gone out with briefly after you. She came in and cooked me a meal for my birthday and really looked after me. I don't know what I would have done without her. (But I needed a much stronger personality). My sister fumed that she was: <u>only 36!</u>

A <u>sacrificial dagger</u>.

Some <u>'liquid' chloroform</u> I had bought on the Internet without any serious intentions. I had money to burn in those days! What an idiot.

I received six months in custody for sending the 'book of poetry' to you father.

I received eighteen months for the time when Benji saw me closing the door from upstairs.

I received two years for the firearm business, but was told I would only serve half.

My Solicitor's Secretary said: "What do you think of that? You will be out in March." I was greatly relieved.

'Two years in prison (and I <u>was forced to serve the full two years in prison</u>, even though I was released to a hostel at the half-way stage): for having a firearm I only had because I felt depressed.' It could only happen to me.

I was banned from 'Wales,' and the whole of Oxfordshire for life.

Just after my confinement began I was being interviewed by one of the Probation gang. I noticed on my file that I was being labelled as a 'Rapist.' I asked them what that was doing on my file. It was never removed as far as I know...

The paintings I had done for you, because they were deemed 'evidence,' were destroyed, along with my books of poetry, after the pigs had smeared them with their greasy genitals. A lot of my property disappeared or was pinched by someone. I ended up with nothing. The museum fire-arm, which had cost me more than £500 to end my life with, was given to the Chief Inspector to see what he could get at auction. I was employed in soul-destroying tasks like 'penny-washing,' or counting t-bags. Those days in prison were the worse of my life. I watched men slash their arms or jump over the balcony because they'd had a 'Dear John,' from the wife.

# The bigger picture

'Let's get this clear! Once and for all.' I snapped.

'One phone call.' 'One text message' (disputed)...

My key worker ploughed on with his pen,

That mighty brain of his doing over-time.

'We have to look at the bigger picture!' he smirked.

'You are dangerous, a menace to society,

and a MAPPA level 3.'


*I felt you thinking about me when you held some of my artwork, and when you found my woolly hat. The one you all laughed at me wearing in Malta. The second jug wasn't as nice as the first one though. It's face wasn't as expressive. I could also feel your mother's sadness despite what she might have said about allowing me into the house...or me being the wrong class of person. The Fuzz informed me that your family didn't want anything to do with me.'*

## The Newton enquiry

I strode to the dock in my *Air-Jordans,*

Pulled by their shifty eyes.

Judge Corrie shrewdly inspected my notes:

"When you wrote that the pigs passed you, In two panda cars...

Did you mean: -the slang for policeman, -a farmyard animal, -

or something else?"

"A farm yard animal!" I replied.

On-the-run.

## Troubadour for the caged nightingale

I'm wondering, If day by day,

As the notes fall by my window,

There will ever be another ray,

Allowed into this void.


As the shrill grey sky shrouds the unforgiving plain of land,

Bare and bootless, Untenanted,

Hollow with a vacant fog.


The whirring Sun,

Glides like a water lily,

Into the creek.

While dying nightly on my steed of silver light.

Shortly before I was released from prison a really nasty man, who was there on some very serious charges, attacked me from behind in a dark corridor, because he said I owed him a 'mars-bar.' It took me a while to get him down and restrain him, but by that time he had hit me with something in my face and blood was spurting all over the corridor and walls.

One of the Guards said she had never seen so much blood in her life.
I was in a terrible state and made a mess in my trousers...
I nearly passed out.
Against the advice of the 'Governor' I called the police in to press charges, but all they did was give him a 'caution.'

# In memory of Michael Hart

At the table: Michael Hart,

gently spoken, moves his piece,

deep in thought, he paces back and forth.

Advances his pawn and protects his Queen,

upon the field of battle,

Takes a bishop with his horse,

sends his rooks above ground.


Chafing his head, he stands,

tall and strong,

fair and pale,

then shakes my hand.

Leaving the room,

beaten but not resigned,

surveying the landscape of his cell,

leaving this world,

his sibling and his life.


The Officers played tricks on me all the time. I could hear them cheering when they locked me away at night. Always complaining about work conditions! A lot of fellows went crazy in there. I cannot sleep in garments. As you know I haven't slept in them for years. I wrapped my thin green sheet around me on my bed, but struggled to relax. Eventually I awoke in the middle of the night. I was woken by the sound of the grill on the door being slammed. The next day I was up in front of the Governor (there were several of them claiming to be 'Governor') for 'exposure.' Apparently one of the Screws had looked through my cell door during the night and had seen me sleeping naked. My sheet must have accidentally slipped off. I was ordered to wear pyjamas at night or face disciplinary proceedings and be put on 'basic.' My mum wrote in to say that I should agree to be incarcerated in a psychiatric establishment for the rest of my life. She wasn't the only one to try and persuade me to sign on the dotted line and surrender my freedom forever...I was warned that if my behaviour didn't improve at once I would be shipped out to somewhere *really nasty* without my feet ever touching the floor. The staff took it out on anyone who showed an ounce of wit or intelligence.
My only recompense was winning the Darts and Scrabble tournaments. I moved into the semi-finals at Chess, but when I won my opponent asked for a re-match, because he said he hadn't been feeling very well on the day. Because I wouldn't play him again his name was put forward into the next round.

You said in one of your statements that you thought you were going up-the-wall. You are lucky. You were barking already!

When I came out of prison they sent me to Milton Keynes. They told me I couldn't talk to any women without their permission because I was too 'dangerous'. If I was ever found with fireworks in my car I would face ten years under their watchful and excellent care! I went to a beautician without telling them (I could have been recalled). When I saw a woman up at the shops with the same mouth and nose as you it made me feel very sad. A year in prison was a very long time to me *and I didn't even suffer from Asperger's*. Roger gave me some book tokens he had just received for his birthday on the day I was released, and took me for a curry. That's the same Roger you said you didn't like because he was a 'Railway anorak!' When I came back from spending the book tokens in town the police were waiting for me back at the hostel, and tried to charge me with something I had not done. The CCTV in the book shop confirmed my story. When I eventually moved to a hostel in Norwich I was disciplined for having a map in my room. The Probation staff at the hostel let everyone know that I was a 'rapist.' I was training to be a 'Spiritual healer' at a nearby church when I met a really pretty lady in her early thirties called <u>Cristina,</u> a local businesswoman. She had a First-class honours in literature, and could speak four languages fluently. She had grown up in Portugal but looked and sounded 'Swedish.' I was extremely proud of her...The staff at the hostel reported me, and the police shoats were due to recall me, for walking her back to her car one night, and for being ten minutes late returning to the hostel, so I went on-the-run. I drove across to Ireland to pick up a caravan and then over to Banbury. I received a free membership at the new gym in the town centre just after Christmas. ~Eventually I returned to Wallingford. It all felt so surreal. I let myself in by the usual methods. When I returned to the camp-site I saw a police car in the distance. In spite of me using my cousin's name as an alias I thought they must have tracked me down. I almost broke my arm trying to run across a muddy field in the darkness and ended up with a lot of cuts and bruises.

# Expulsion of the crack-brained flea

I was sent home today,
Not because I did anything wrong,
back to the shell of grey moths,
which looks like an elderly rail-carriage.

The ferric grille of death and bird-dung,
my one-legged cell-mate,
who stands over me as I eat,
chattering incessantly,
about Cud'orth,
cockney Steve and Joan, And Charlie Williams.
Can't even remember what day it is.

Back to the rigid jar of Ovaltine,
my box of pens, my jug, and my stash of jams.
To the squalid little rhymes,
the adamant bed, nailed to the floor,
The Sun-shuffling blogs, attempting to shed some daylight,
on all this cheerless indignation.

Back to the skids on my bedsheets,
the black pin-heads on my pillow,
the caves in my mattress...
Back to my pad and my toothpaste,
The notice-board stuffed with unrepeatable slang.
To my home without a key, bolted on the outside.
Because the teacher, didn't want to be,
in the same room as me, alone,
    Unseasonably sent forward.

# Astonished by the softness I feel

Our hands embraced,
All through the service...
This is wrong she whispered,
You are very bad.

As we ran through the rain our fingers touched,
This is wicked Andrew,
And you mustn't!

Her voice rang out like a church-bell in the tender heart of the city,
On the cold grey seat where we huddled.
With eyes as big as saucers she spoke of childhood tresses,
Her dainty shoes,
Like two white mice,
Gleaming,
And hearing every word.

Are you a gunrunner,
Do you have a deal to make,
Why do you keep running off like that,
Why do you have to go so suddenly,
Andrew?

Bitterness like cast-iron,
Unforgiving, brittle, and light,
Unsparing.
My hand sank like a leaf to her skirt.
No one knew poetry like she did.

You left a postcard to Rose from your holiday in Benidorm, in the kitchen. I did wonder why your escort had signed it 'G. Mills.' Very formal? I don't know how I didn't wake you all up slamming the door so hard. The next time I went over you were in the kitchen for ages, toying with your hair, while you gabbed on the phone. I was getting very bored, and it was bluddy cold out in that garden. The spikes on the wall were no deterrent: I flew over them!

It felt so strange seeing you Elizabeth. You'd hardly changed, but your hair looked a bit lighter. You were always asking people if they preferred blondes.

Benji and Emily came in and out of the room several times. I guess they were about ready for bed. Emily went to switch my telly and video off. The cat was no-where to be seen. I hope he hadn't died.

I wasn't sure if I had been seen, but Benji went to fetch your new lodger and got her to look out into the garden. He pointed towards the window, but that was all. She went back upstairs. Then I saw you hide behind the door with a very mischievous grin, peeping round it, as they all went up to bed. You didn't seem aware of my presence. You scolded them up to bed.

You plonked yourself down on your computer chair with a glass of wine in one hand and a bottle in the other.

You pretended to peer round the door, and then very naughtily shoved both hands into your trousers. You made some really suggestive faces as you looked at the screen. Unfortunately, I was unable to see what was on it in spite of standing in the corner with my binoculars. You simulated sex and appeared very raunchy. You were wearing your tweed trousers and you had your glasses on. Your middle area looked a bit loose and paunchy.

Emily came to watch you and stood by your side. You nodded at the screen. She stood for a short while and then went out and shut the door...good for her! I was so sorry for you. I didn't know what to do. I have never seen anything so sad in all my life.

I could have cried. I think I did shed a few tears watching you.

Your hand went in and out all the time. Sometimes you just lolled in a stupor. You appeared to be communicating with someone and typing with great difficulty and deliberation.

After a while your glasses fell off and you slumped in your chair, with your belly extended and your shirt sticking out.

You seemed to be slurring your speech.

Benji came down from upstairs. He sat on the couch behind you, pretending to be asleep. He kept sneaking a look into the garden (God knows how he knew I was there) and then back at you, at what you were doing. You were masturbating in front of your own children again. This went on for several minutes. Benji kept arching a bit closer and tried to peer over your shoulder to see what you were looking at.

You kept wafting your hand at him, as if to say he had to stay put, and you couldn't help what you were doing.

I suppose he must have been about twelve by this time, although he still wasn't very tall.

Then he got up and went.

You spilt your wine.

Your trousers were split.

When you dropped your glasses, you started to squint at the screen and your head tottered backwards and forwards.

Then you suddenly got up and went to bed.

Am I mad to think I should have been there with you in person?

I left Emily some presents, which I know she opened.

I felt uneasy the next week. As if someone was thinking about me. I thought it was the u-know-who's. I always have a sixth sense about filth. Driving across I felt very troubled. I even passed a panda car leaving Didcot. I parked my car up the road and walked down. The field and woods had changed a little.... I stood on a large tree-trunk on the other side of the road. The farmland had been cleared.

When I reached the jumping wall, I knew something was wrong.

You were all huddled together on the sofa. You looked absolutely petrified and on the edge of breaking down. I felt utterly miserable about that. I can never tell you how sorry I am. It wasn't your fault that my life had turned out such a mess...

I could not resist sending you a message as I stood in the corner, on the spur of the moment. It was very foolish of me. I am very sorry for using the C-word. I meant to write *hairy bush*. It sounded very crude, and I never liked to be crude with you. That's when you tried to ring me. I saw you toying with a white pencil between your lips and looking for some details: probably the Eustace fellow's. It was the only sex-text I ever sent you in my life.

You herded the children upstairs, flicked the lights off, and went to lie on the back-hall floor, peeking through the cat-flap. I hardly dared to breath. I knew if I were caught there I would be in serious trouble. I was surprised after what I had seen that you told anyone. I knew the cops had arrived, but I couldn't move until you went upstairs.

I was only just able to get away, as they came around the corner with a police dog, by crawling over the road, and leap-frogging a barbed-wire fence. I cut my hand scaling a seven-foot wall...Not bad for an old-timer! Afterall, my new nickname was: 'dare-devil.' I rang the house when I reached a safe distance, and said I was sorry and never meant to hurt you. Benji answered the phone. The policeman put on a funny voice pretending to be you. I could have left the area but it had been snowing and I didn't really know where to go.

I knew they were after me. When I was followed coming back from the bike-shop the next day I knew my number was up.

They dragged me from my car even though I wanted to come peacefully. I was so petrified that I actually called for my mother. I could hardly breathe and I thought they were going to kill me. They kept calling me the most repulsive names and thumping me. They told me that if I ever returned to Oxfordshire again they would: "hunt me down!" One officer held a gun to my head.

You said in your statement that you had to go to the doctor because of me, and that Benji had to too. I am sorry if I added to your problems but <u>you were seeing the doctor long before me.</u> You made it sound as if I was the source of all your difficulties. You blamed me for almost everything. You said you were afraid of what I would do next and that I might ruin your life...You said that you knew it was me who sent you the text message because I was always sending you explicit messages, which wasn't true. You told the court that you were afraid I was going to commit a serious sexual offence against you, which as you probably knew was absolute rubbish. You told the court that you were afraid of appearing in person because you thought I might attack you...!

You told the court you didn't want to appear in person because you thought I might get too turned on if I heard your voice. I used to walk away from the phone sometimes because your voice was so boring and monotonous.

I don't know if anyone has ever told you, but prison is not a joke, and it isn't funny. It can turn you into a complete wreck.

When I received another sentence of two and half years it was a terrible shock. I received an extra year for not notifying the police of my 'change of address......!' Eustace gleamed at me across the Courtroom. He bragged about visiting you forty or fifty times. He said the kids always came running to see him and that he had never seen a wine bottle in sight. The Judge believed him. Probably just *trying* to make me 'jealous.'

# Too many questions Mr Chawla

How did we manage,
Yes, we are locked up,
Do I have a sister?
Will we be allowed home for Christmas…
What time is it,
Do we have a panic button,
Is my name Irish?
Mr Chawla.

Maybe these joggers,
Do have elasticated bottoms,
Have I ever been skiing in the Himalayas,
Do I remember Britt Ekland?
Mr Chawla.

Did my grandfather fight at Dunkirk,
What are we having tomorrow,
Does the Queen pay for the poppies?
And yes, I do remember the little man in Benny Hill,
Mr Chawla.

I represented *myself* over the phone call business, even though I was
in such a terrible state and very out-of-sorts: no breakfast, no
shower, and no sleep.  The Screws were in stitches taking me down
to Court. I was handcuffed in the van, and ordered to give back my
pencil.  I was charged with contacting you on the phone (on my
birthday), thereby breaking a 'restraining order.'
The only evidence they had was a discarded SIM-card on the floor
of my Hilux. I could so easily have been tossed it out of the window.
"I'm sorry, but I never meant to hurt you!" How is that threatening?
I was referring to the broken museum fire-arm which I had
intended to end my life with, which was not about you at all.
I admitted contacting you on the phone, but that was not enough
for the Authorities. I had to go to a 'Newton' enquiry to make it

sound even worse than it was, so they could get me a far worse sentence. The Prosecuting Barrister read all the text message out, slowly emphasizing every word. The poxy old Faggot gaped in in *disbelief*. At subsequent hearings it was deemed so disgusting that it could not even be heard in open court. I believe the message contained some references to *black vibrators* and multiple orgasms. The Prosecution dredged up every horrid little detail they could from the past. They tried to make me look as bad as possible but I suppose that's what they get paid to do. It was all very one-sided. They weren't interested to know that you still had some of my property, and they believed your statement that our relationship was never intimate, that you had only known me a few days, and that I had stalked you until you had to have psychiatric treatment and were in fear of your life. In Court your name fluctuated between: 'Mrs Mills, Miss Farley-hills, and 'Mrs Strange.' *Eustace* wrote in his statement that I had sworn at him on the phone which I certainly did not. My impotence was cited.

My former employers couldn't believe the severity of my sentence. Neither did they think I deserved the label given me by the police and the media thanks to you. The papers labelled me as a monster. My second sentence was even worse than the first.

## The mighty brawn of Michael Connolly

There was a lad, called Michael Connolly,
there was a time, I knew him well.
I didn't think, I'd ever want to be,
without his might, his will, his strength.

I know he could,
I've seen him easily,
bear a truck,
Lift up a dwelling place.

He even stood,
between me and Mullaney,
I miss him now, like a blue sea.

ALL ENTRIES ON THIS PAGE TO BE TYPEWRITTEN    Custody No.

Station ..... ABINGDON

FULL NAME ..... B̶LANDFORDHOOK ..... Date of Birth ..... 02/02/956

Address .....

"You are charged with the offence(s) shown below. You do not have to say anything. But it may harm your defence if you do not mention now something you later rely on in court. Anything you say may be given in evidence".

Charge(s)

> On 02/02/09 at WALLINGFORD in the County of Oxfordshire without reasonable excuse you contacted Elizabeth FARLEYHILLS by text message and by telephone when you were prohibited from doing by a restraining order imposed by Oxford Crown Court on 27/07/2007 [inets 4 all]. Contrary to Section 5 (5) and (6) of the Protection from Harassment Act 1997.

*Obscure. Need more details before plea
What text message? Which number to?
By phone when?*

*① Struck by circumstances ② Original incident*
*ⓐ victim & rehabilitated — letter of apology — exp not ind*
*ⓑ Had a prev. warning for coming back late*

*bad*

*⚡ Threats of danger*

Reply to Charge(s) .....

Person Charging ..... 6/Con ..... 733368
(Include Rank & Number)

Time & date charged .1015 ..... 4/3/09

Officer ACCEPTING THE CHARGE .....
(Signature, Rank & Number)

Officer in case .. DS/KIEMENC
Name, Rank & No. (In Block Capitals)

(if bailed s. 47(3) P.A.C.E. Act 1984, specify offence(s) being enquired into) (If on warrant, quote date and Court of issue)

I acknowledge that I have received a written copy of the Charge(s), *Bail Record, *Legal aid, *Notice to Indicate Plea, *Statutory notification of Advance Disclosure Entitlement.

I had to serve the remainder of the first sentence along with this new sentence, and also all the time I spent 'at-large'.

# I fear that Ishmael's head may still be shrinking

I fear that Ishmael's head may still be shrinking,
And it wasn't too big to begin with.
I fear that the staff,
Are stealing in at night;
Removing the brilliant substance of his thoughts.
I fear that Ishmael's head may still be shrinking,
He's tall and thin,
And soon he'll be all gone.
But that leaves his *indeterminate sentence*,
A long one, we can all rest assured.

I don't know how I ever got through it all. It completely wore me out. I was told that I was a 'Sex-offender.' I asked them why I was not on the Sex-offender's Register then? They told me that I *was a* 'Sex-offender,' only one who was not on the Register, and thus began my incessant flitting from cell to cell. I was ordered to move all my belongings four times a day. On one occasion I was put in solitary confinement for wearing the wrong kind of trousers. The Officers poked fun at me and wanted to know if I had ever been sectioned. I was forced back from the exercise yard for having a pair of boots on my feet. I couldn't eat the food because of what they put in it. I had a hunch they were masturbating in my food so I wouldn't touch it. Jenny at the hostel told me I looked younger than the men who were younger than me, whatever that meant. The gym mirror declared how broken I was. I looked in the mirror one day and for the first time in my life noticed my arms sagging. My face was grey and awful. I was changing into an old man! Probation said that if there was any sexual content at all in my text message (which could have been sent by a chimpanzee at London Zoo), then I would never hear the end of it...!

# Stalker

On safari,
in the library,
Over field and into dale,
He pursued us without warning,
Kept us captive in our home.
We were frightened by his presence,
At the kerbside when it rang,
When he reached, as if to follow,
We were shaking, as we ran.

We were certain, that he meant harm,
We were taught, that he could kill,
That's before they found him floating,
In the river all alone...

Dragged up from the very water,
Caked in weed and seed and mud,
Round his eyes the scorch of sorrow,
Daddy was a working man.

I recall now, on the blanket,
Summer picnics, on the grass,
He was always in a temper,
But he carried us to bed.

I was attacked by someone suffering from schizophrenia in the middle of the night. He was smashing up the cell when I awoke. He said he was going to kill me. The man had a long history of 'indecent exposure.' I rang the alarm bell but no-one came. By the time help arrived he had smashed the table over me and scratched the top of my head with his fingers. The next day the Officers smirked at me over the table.

"So how did you know he was suffering from schizophrenia, are you a fucking expert?"

"Because he told me himself, and because I once worked in mental health," I said.

It just seemed to go on and on forever. When I eventually walked through the gate a police car was waiting for me. The Screws were roaring with laughter, because that usually meant you were going to be re-arrested for something else. Once again, I had to sign the Register at the hostel every hour, or I would be immediately recalled, even if I was sick in my room. After a few months of relative 'freedom' I was recalled for going on a library computer to do a job search, <u>even though I didn't contact anyone I was told not to,</u> and had to spend another humiliating and tortuous year inside.

## Wore a *white* T-shirt

I was pursued, Into my class today,
With angry glares and the downcast eye.
Hasty phone calls were made,
Guards were waiting for me on the stairs.
The sneers of fellow in-mates,
Across the landing,
Foul language,
From appalled and high-class kitchen staff,
And the boorish unrefined,
Wearing only blue.


I was sent to HMP ******* where I went on the main wing, but had urine and even more unpleasant things thrown through my door. Some of the young men said the most revolting things to me.

They threatened to slash my throat and even tried to set fire to my cell. My mum never came in to see me. She said she had a toothache and that all sex-offenders should be castrated. I wouldn't have wanted to see her anyway. All my family disowned me. *Pam and Howard* offered to drive over to see me from Oxford every week. They were both in their seventies but very supportive. I couldn't help asking: what had I really done to deserve all this?

## 'A former work colleague saw me in line with the local hobos awaiting my food hand-out'

I eventually passed through my sentence with the assistance of an old nun from Rome. Each week we prayed in a small religious group at church. We passed a lighted candle round the room and spoke about our feelings. I was the only one in the room not on a 'life-sentence.' A Spiritualist who came in to see me said that it was very hard for him to feel any love in a place like that. By the time I was released again I was practically a zombie. I *had* managed to avoid taking any drugs for depression because they only made you worse! Some of the ass-bandits even tried to get me to do things with them. The State tried to keep me in the system forever.

'The police stopped me from taking part in a Writer's group and from attending the church. I was commanded not to go near any women or to wear my riding shorts. I was not allowed to travel into London to receive my National award for poetry or to speak before a gathering of dignitaries, including MP's and the Head of Probation, although I do understand that some of my work was heard on the BBC. With that kind of 'freedom' I might easily have picked up a phone and tried to contact you again. For years I dreamt about going back to the house. The dreams were always the same. I found myself wandering a cobbled street in the dead of night. It went up-hill between a lot of shops and buildings. Then I would be in a dimly lit lane...sometimes I was on some stairs, with you talking in another room. At other times I found myself in an unknown house during the day time, while you were out at work. My restless soul haunted the places you lived.'

**'I had to sign a document to say that if I bought any fire-works I would be imprisoned for up to ten years'**

The Authorities warned everyone that I was a _dangerous psychopath_ and that no-one could feel safe with me in the area.

They poked their noses into everything I did. I wasn't allowed to do anything without their say so. I wasn't allowed to make any meaningful friendships. My sister and mother were told the most spiteful and prejudiced nonsense. As if they needed any encouragement. After several attempts I finally settled into a flat for the elderly, after being evicted from the Probation hostel and made homeless because my probation period had run out, and I was no longer on any kind of licence. But the Residents had already been warned about me before I arrived so they were already in a mood to loathe me...wonderful sympathetic human beings!

## A Scarecrow of shipwrecked violins

Saffron-shyed and curry-combed,
I wavered to the bed,
on a tattered pole of moor-hawks,
lunge-whipped and saddle-worn.

Whipple tree'd and haggled with,
goat sea-stormed, and curb-bit freed.
Breech-band stringed on nine-foot stilts,
hip-strapped, with magpie-geese.

Throat-latch curled, and buttress-winged,
cure-rain-bent and nose-bleed-pommelled,
brindled in rags and low cantled.

Just before I returned from perdition the Fuzz applied for a SOPO order, because that was the end of my sentence, and I was not on the Sex-offender's register. They applied for it just so they could keep tabs on me and so they could interfere in everything I did. They told the Court that I was in danger of attacking my former partner or a member of the public and committing a serious sexual offence against them. They also labelled me as being a danger to children. When I stood up for myself and said that this was absolute nonsense and that I had split up with my ex-girlfriend because I didn't want to touch her, even when we slept in the same room, I was accused of being aggressive.

The Magistrates peered down their snooty noses at me.

No doubt my goose had already been cooked long before I even appeared in the dock. The Pigs were grinning from ear to ear to see my name added to the ever-growing list of "wrong-uns."

Having a SOPO gave them immediate access to my home and the power to have me thrown into prison quicker than a Politician knows how to run. I was harassed by the pigs wherever I went and had my bedroom turned over on many occasions. My writing was removed and my artwork classified as 'threatening,' just because one of my paintings contained a nude picture of a woman. Something I had done in a life-class, while completing my honours degree in Fine Art. In truth my nightmare was only just beginning. The idea had been to shunt me from pillar to post until they could find another reason to lock me up again. I was warned that if someone heard me swearing or using foul language I would be thrown in the back of a panda car and never heard of again.

All the Public saw was my label and where I came from.

I was forced to sign a declaration that I would inform anyone with whom I made contact or with whom I tried to form a new relationship about my past.

I tried to run a coffee morning for older people but the police were always appearing through the side-doors.

I had a bucket of water thrown over me at the Christmas party. Police cars escorted me wherever I travelled. My e-mails were dissected and my post tampered with on a regular basis. Relatives I'd known all my life refused to visit if I was around. I was chased by a mob from the Job-Centre right across town. I tried to get over to Ireland to make a 'new-start,' but the police were waiting for me at the other side with a slip of paper to sign: <u>that I was a 'Sex-offender.'</u>

The police from this side of the Irish sea informed me that had I not returned within one day they would have had to go on searching for me for years until they could finally return me to jail.

My new girlfriend kept asking: "Why can't they leave us alone?" After ten years of this I'm sick to death. I totally reject their description of me!

I do apologise for not being able to tell you all this in person AND FOR MY POOR HANDWRITING...

ORIGINAL STORY WRITTEN 2009-11. Edited, tweaked, and up-dated February 2018. (Awaiting knee-replacements and heart-by-pass).

# Guerdon of the orange Snowman

Here among the dead-men, covered in black slime,
bottom of the bunker, smothered in faint rose...
It's dread among the hopeless, the ceiling sharp with ice,
slipping with the moonbeams, falling on chill hearts.

The stiff corpse of the swallow,
freezing on the gravel,
shivers at my cell-door,
droned in spits of red.

In the forest of the Snowman,
together with lost fires,
the bowl is huge and endless,
forever for all time.

In the forest of the Snowman,
there's heaven in the flame,
giving to the meeting, alive alive alive...!

You get there through the Autumn,
you get there through the heart,
where rivers are in torrent,

and true-love never dies.

# Held accountable for blushing

If it were a sin,

then I would walk on hot coals forever,

passing each cloud, as if it were a seething spring.

Shunning each intimate moment,

Steering clear from every place, where people dwell.

Seeing each hall, as if it were a Court of law,

harming every sunlit waterfall, and haven.

# The dog's bollocks

She sings his praises,
every time they pet,
in the Visitor's den,
where her cleavage, spills,
and his fingers molest the hem of her skirt.

Martin Fungus preens himself in the steely square,
of the cell mirror,
squirting Clearasil on his flaking skin,
wires of dark hair moulting everywhere:
"You really are the dog's bollocks!" I yelped.

An alien life-form attempted to elope, from his neck,
His bare arms protruded with a leviathan of blades,
something unpleasant erupted from behind an ear:
"The dog's bollocks!" I yelled.
"Another innocent man locked up in jail!"
I slapped the desk in disgust.

He stared impassively, like a heap of vanilla,
a nest of love-bites encroaching on his chest:
"Dog's bollocks!" I said.

"Just because I wouldn't give her any more money, for
drugs," he enunciated.
"Bollocks!" I said.
"It'll cost them an arm and a leg when you appeal."

A reptilian leer.

# biography

Born in West Yorkshire, son of an English Schoolteacher and an Irish wolfhound.
Worked as an Art therapist, British Rail Signalman, and teacher of Sign-language.
Currently runs a creative writing workshop in Norfolk.
Award winning poet and short story writer.
Trained Astrologer and former body-builder.
Social Commentator of world-renown. Magic carpet restorer. Campaigner for Tourette's.
In 2007 was caught in possession of a First World War Browning revolver which had once
belonged to Field Marshal Erwin Rommel, but did not intend to murder anyone with it.
Once taught Boris Johnson how to throw a welly.
Staunch believer in Universal freedom; the obligation to question, especially those with received
authority, and the rights of the individual over and above that of the State.
Strong opponent of political correctness and Government eunuchs with the upper storey missing.

\* BARRED FROM LIBRARIES AND DOSS CENTRES UP AND DOWN THE COUNTRY.

Also by the same Author: Hrothgar's lost parchments, Thunderbuck Ram I and II:
(The 'Changeling,' Eye of the Medusa, Grendel Returns, Fimbulwinter).
Dada's final Gallery. Dance of the red-crowned Prince.
BUNDERCHOOK STARWORD POET:  Odd bent Coppers, Natural Surveillance, Trades of the
Toadman, Widening Underground, Offensive behaviour, Alien Intelligence, Criminal Tendencies.
Bunderchook Starword Poet 'Revival': Philistines, Angels and Queers.

## Dear *LIBRARY OF WALES,*

**Thank you for handing my book straight to the Plebs.  It was very public spirited of you!**
Llanfairpwllgwyngyllgogerychwyrndrobwllllantysiliogogogoch.

# Belinda's hot air

**Let me get this right! By Ginger Vitus Published February 11 2018 Edit**

The Manager of a well-known charity on an overseas island pays someone for sex. I don't know if this was in place of food or fire-arms; whether it was just an employee of the company or a wandering Samaritan? Moral do-gooders and 'improvers' of mankind seem to think that 'exploitation,' aggression and greed are something we could all do without. That one day the world will be a better place when it is finally eradicated from our planet. Paying for sex, either in food, hospitality or a promise of a career break, is fine by me!

\* When I was growing up you could walk through the local council estate and get anything you wanted with a packet of peanuts.

# FACEBOOK BLOG

'I just wanted to say something about how the Authorities, encouraged by Government, who are making an even more concerted effort to dismantle and control the Inter-net, so we can all be forced to sing from the same frigging hymn sheet. Governments are generally infected with morality, so anarchic thoughts are just too much for them to bear. The truth behind their methods and how to deal with them are in my books of satire: 'BUNDERCHOOK STARWORD POET'. To close the inter-net down and put it under state control would severely curtail your ability to express an opinion. How long before we are forced to have cameras pointed into our living-rooms? We can't all be goody-two-shoes!'

## Affordable housing By GODFREY WINKLEBACKER | Published: JANUARY 31, 2018

Our Green belt land is gradually being swallowed up by an ever-increasing population. The excuse for this is that it provides essential housing for homeless people, and for foreign migrants. How the hell is anyone like that going to afford homes that are hundreds of thousands each and land which is worth one million pounds per acre? Governments could of course, provide them free if they wanted. Governments can do anything they like with the law on their side. Anything except LISTEN!

# Doing all I can By Bird Dung Published February 15 2018 Edit

*Pain-in-the-butt.*

Mum has started calling the cat "Keith!" Sam doesn't look anything like Keith. She is still loading things into the wrong bins and planting plastic flowers in the garden.

*'Someone once asked me why I was still alive many years ago. They wanted to know why I hadn't been killed already. Apparently, I was always upsetting people by the things I said'*

1Stephen PLO Israel

Thumbs up!

**Comments**
View 1 more comment

Mohammed Hafty For real this it you know why coz when you take care about peaple they will say that you're stupid fucking emptty mind and deeply they do know nothing.

Drew Gallagher Why, thank you kind Sir!

Manage FACEBOOK.

Mette Fuglsang von Hessen Nuremberg

If ppl don't ask or ask u to stop, you STOP ! Doesn't make them stupid empty minded ! A man who are obsessed w a woman engaged to a famous actor, and keeps on making sexual innuendo, THATS empty minded and stupid !! I then try to be sweet and tell how my bf just bought me a 4000$ Valentino dress and he doesn't even answer. THATS rude ! And not friendship at all !!

Manage

Well I'm sorry to say so but you still say very inappropriate things on chats , sexual things though I am deeply involved w another man . That's not ok and I tell u to stop my bf even asked u to. I block u then take u back and u continue to talk about wanting pics w my hands under my shirt making me feel like a whore. U stressed me to the point when sick that I tragically lost my baby being ill already and all I was told was I couldn't stress yet u kept pestering me to can talk for hours and I said no ! U kept on until I began bleeding! So honestly , those who don't see this side of you where u have NO filter or remorse of what happened .... I think for one Bob Nothing-in-bed, who is a common friend will be on my side!

I don't even know what you mean but as I wrote: if you say things like that you force me to block you so can you not do this ?! Drew I let u back though I lost my baby mainly bc of you, **that's what the doctors said...**

What do you think of me now?                          Drew Gallagher ?

83

# Relationship abuse

By ADUMLA | *Published: FEBRUARY 25, 2018*

We are now in an age where relationships can be case-managed and Government eunuchs can appoint staff to monitor our performance:

- gangs of interfering super-nannies
- the use of drugs like warfarin ok!
- fit young professional snoops
- made to feel very special
- mistrust of the State
- missed childhood experiences

# Lazy pigs!

By USULI TWELVES | *Published: FEBRUARY 23, 2018* | *Edit*

After the theft of my lovely Cannondale bicycle on Monday I contacted the pigs to say it was in all likelihood taken by a pair of hoodies, laying in wait at the fish shop. It isn't the only bicycle that's been stolen in town.

They told me I had better check all the CCTV footage in the area.

I reminded them it was *their* duty to check their own surveillance cameras, which are pasted on every lamp-post and building from here to kingdom come. Today they wrote back to say they were closing the case and that there was nothing more they could do. Pillocks! Oh, sorry, you can get arrested for swearing these days in this fair and tolerant land...okay. Doofus!

# Dorkus again

By USULI TWELVES | *Published: FEBRUARY 23, 2018* | *Edit*

"You should be happy just being with me!"

But Emmerdale is a load of cow's bollocks!

# End of the planet

By USULI TWELVES | *Published: FEBRUARY 23, 2018* | *Edit*

In a dream this morning I saw a huge meteor, which looked like a burning planet, enter our atmosphere in the distance. I prayed to god that it would pass us by and land a million miles away. Instead it crashed down just beside us and exploded in a white misty spray. My sister was there. Then there was silence!

# Loose Women too

By GODFREY WINKLEBACKER | *Published: FEBRUARY 21, 2018* | *Edit*

It was no surprise to see an old footballer on Loose Women moaning about the past. Best take advantage of the present public hysteria. He didn't like any of it, he said. When I was growing up there were always a few strange men about. Some of my friends were assaulted by them at the age of twelve or thirteen. I was very wary and kept my distance. It sounded horrendous.

One of them was a very well-known local Scout Master. For months he tried to get me on my own. I wasn't stupid. The last time I saw him was at the Annual Christmas Fair in town. I saw him with his fat accomplice standing near the dodgem cars, in his beret. I hadn't seen him for months. My mum had asked him to stop calling at our house. When he saw me he waved and started walking towards me. I ran like hell into the crowds.

I was shaking like a proverbial leaf. I suppose they will all be dead by now.

After receiving the customary applause, the footballer left the table, and on walked Will Young with his new boyfriend. I heard he started very young.

Very popular with the audience!

## Elementary my dear Watson…!
*By ADUMLA | Published: FEBRUARY 25, 2018 | Edit*

The new series, 'Troy,' has been a brilliant success.  Drawing on a variety of ancient sources it really makes you feel as if you know the central characters, and their human frailties.   Gods and elemental forces become part of the whole framework.  Their presence is realistic and true to life, representing universal archetypes familiar to us all.  One small error:  Odysseus was not in fact called 'Odysseus,' until he returned home.  Before that he was simply known as 'Ulysses,' and Helen was not the face that sailed a thousand ships, but the face that .ucked a thousand .ocks!  A mistake made by Christian scholars when interpreting their manuscript many many centuries ago.

### Trannies bankrupting the Health Service
By GODFREY WINKLEBACKER | Published: FEBRUARY 22, 2018 |
If you say anything horrid I will cry and make a face
I love wearing rouge and looking good in high heels
Upsetting someone isn't nice! I will go and report you!
Anyone calling themselves a man will be severely punished
By 2100 there will be 100 different kinds of gender
The numbers go up more quickly than the Cops when counting bullets
ALL GENDER PISSING SHED.

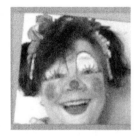

## Money money money
*By GODFREY WINKLEBACKER | Published: FEBRUARY 22, 2018 | Edit*

Women are finding it hard to manage a career as well as look after a family. You can always stay at home if you don't like it!

## .I wouldn't give a poncy old Judge…
*By PETER SMITH | Published: FEBRUARY 20, 2018 | Edit*

the steam off my shower head, even if the whole world collapsed.
Handing out fines for swearing.
Members of the Establishment!  Who give's a truck…

# HEADWOOD

## A reward of £50 to anyone coming forward with information leading to the recovery of my precious Cannondale.

S T O L E N: White Cannondale Mountain bike

At about five thirty on Monday evening (19th February) a white mountain bike was stolen from outside Bonds fish and chip shop (next to the dry cleaners) on Red Lion Street, in Aylsham.

## Wanted:
in connection with the incident:
• two white males in hoodies
• aged about 17/20
• wearing light greenish clothing
• pale complexion short or shaven hair
• slim, about six foot tall
Seen in the premises shortly before, and smoking weed!

## Fifty shades of pink

By PETER SMITH | *Published: FEBRUARY 18, 2018* | *Edit*

An over-hyped piece of crap!

## Most boring over-rated act on telly…

By USULI TWELVES | *Published: FEBRUARY 16, 2018* | *Edit*

You've guessed it!  Olly 'I'll do anything to get on telly' Murs.

## GIRL POWER

By USULI TWELVES | *Published: FEBRUARY 16, 2018* | *Edit*

I watched Siobhan turn up at her ex-s on Corrie tonight, half naked, forcibly snog him (when he didn't want anything to do with her), push him onto his bed and wrap her legs around him, before having sex.  In this new, wonderfully-fair world we now live in, a man behaving like this would be labelled as a *sexual predator* and would be immediately arrested.

**Men are wicked!** *By USULI TWELVES | Published: FEBRUARY 16, 2018 | Edit*
Any man who makes a 'pass' at a woman is a sexual predator and should be arrested. Say the:
'NATIONAL COUNCIL OF LES B. FRIENDS AND RUG-MUNCHERS'

## Spiderman

*By RUMPLESTILTSKIN | Published: FEBRUARY 16, 2018 | Edit*
Some of the girls were laughing their heads off at the Bure Valley Railway the other day. I was waiting for my partner to come in on the train. Their Manager kept glancing in my direction. When one of the girls went to sit with her grandma in the cafe her grandma asked her what they were all laughing at. She said that someone had seen a big hairy spider in the kitchen.
There are even more gossips in the office.

## The price of retribution

*By RUMPLESTILTSKIN | Published: FEBRUARY 16, 2018 | Edit*
A tear      = 2p
Three tears = £50
Ten tears    = £1000
Cry buckets = as much as you can carry £/$!

## Are Politicians really so dumb…?

*By ADUMLA | Published: FEBRUARY 9, 2018 | Edit*
Selfish, egocentric, unable to make decisions, rich and prosperous, completely impartial to bribes.
Do you really need to ask?

## Written for your chums…

*By ADUMLA | Published: FEBRUARY 9, 2018 | Edit*
In days of yore Producers looked around for an Actor to fill the role: now they write the part _for their friends_ to bask in the glory.
'I just wanted to something about how the Authorities, encouraged by Government, are making an even more concerted effort to break up and control the Inter-net, so we can all be forced to sing from the same frigging hymn sheet. Governments are generally infected with morality, so anarchic thoughts are just too much for them to bear. The truth behind their methods and how to deal with them are in my books of satire: 'BUNDERCHOOK STARWORD POET. To close the inter-net down and put it under state control would alter it dramatically and severely curtail your right to express an opinion. How long before we are forced to have cameras pointed into a living-rooms? We can't all be goody-two-shoes!
MUM
What was more annoying: she had loaded all the wrong things into one of the bins.
I had to empty them into the right one.
The next day they were all back in the wrong bin again!
…has received your card and huge bouquet of flowers from Canada.
They have been lying out in the rain ever since.

## Trump tackles gun crime

*By BIRD DUNG | Published: FEBRUARY 15, 2018 | Edit*
1. Bullying teachers
2. Nasty annoying pupils
3. Peer pressure and aggression
4. Natural competition
5. Nurses in uniform

## Central Adoption Committee

## Dear Mr BUNDERCHOOK,

Your application for adoption has been refused owing to a shortage of willing participants.

ONLY READ THIS IF YOU ARE GRAY

# THE END?

Printed in Great Britain
by Amazon